Generation Griffey: Rankfest

The Ultimate 90s Dude Countdown

Jon Finkel

Meathead Media

Introduction

What is a Rankfest?

Let's start with a quick Q&A:

What is a rankfest?

It's a festival of ranking things in book form. Obviously. Also, I made it up. In this case, we're ranking 90 of our favorite 90s things across 10 categories:

Commercials, Comedies & Comedians, College, Television, Sports & Action Movies, Food, Gear, Personalities, Video Games, Athletes

Why 'Generation Griffey'?

First, it's a great name. We've got alliteration, 'generation' and the quintessential athlete from that era: Ken Griffey Jr... Junior is the perfect person to define the era of late 80s and 90s kids because the apex of his career matches our childhood perfectly. From the day he entered the Mariner's lineup in 1989 through the next decade, nobody typified 90s style (the backwards hat), 90s swagger (the swing, the smile, the commercials) and 90s coolness (the kicks, the cameos, the crossover stardom) like Griffey.

His reign at the top of the sports/celebrity pyramid (with Jordan) from his rookie year in Seattle to when he joined the Reds in 2000 is the perfect bookend for all of us who grew up around the last decade of the last century.

See, Generation Griffey is a spectacular name for this book.

What Are We Ranking?

Everything. Well, not everything, but the 90 most nostalgic things that make us dudes smile all these years later: the movies we quoted, the athletes we loved, the cards we collected, the foods we ate, the shows we watched and more. All of it.

How Are We Ranking Things?

Glad you asked. When we're ranking a list of similar items (movies, athletes, foods, etc…) it's easy. We create several categories, assign them an objective number based on how we evaluated them in that area and… boom… we've got a ranking

However, when it comes to our overall ranking at the end of the book when the things we're ranking are up against each other but have no common traits (like, let's say, Hot Pockets, Barry Sanders and Saved By the Bell) then we need a much looser ratings system that can encompass everything without using an actual concrete number.

After careful consideration, these are the three categories I used as my baseline when considering how I rank every 90s thing:

1) Hold-Up-Ability: Does this thing hold up today? This is a simple question we all ask ourselves when we rewatch a movie or try a food we used to like or watch highlights from thirty years ago: Does this hold up? Do I still like it? Is it still bad ass?

Also, has our collective enjoyment of this person or thing diminished over time because of external factors like technology or a sport changing or culture changing or humor being different or anything like that? That's a secondary thing to consider.

2) Take You Backness: How much does this take you back? This is perhaps the most important category. When you think of this thing/person, are you instantly transported to the 90s? Do you get that same feeling? Does it put a smile on your face? Do you instinctively nod? If 'yes' to all three then we are at peak "take you backness".

3) Modern Influence & Relevance: How much did you quote, mimic, copy, or use this thing back in the day AND does this thing still matter in today's culture? Some things/people had their moment and disappeared; others stand the test of time. The more often that something on this list is still referenced or referred to today, the more weight I'll give that thing in my final consideration.

After coming up with a master list of a few hundred nineties things, I used the categories I mentioned earlier to rank the top 90 overall. I have no doubt you'll find something I egregiously left off and that you'll want to revoke my 90s card for putting something on. I'm a big boy, I can take disagreements. When you're done reading, you can hit me on social media (@JonFinkel) for Twitter/X and Instagram and let me know where I nailed it and where I blew it.

Got it? Good. Let's go.

For all my fellow 90s dudes.

We had it good.

Other Books

By Jon Finkel

Macho Man: The Untamed, Unbelievable Life of Randy Savage

1996: A Biography: Reliving the Legend Packed, Dynasty Stacked Most Iconic Sports Year of All Time

Hoops Heist: Seattle, the Sonics and How a Stolen Team's Legacy Gave Rise to the NBA's Secret Empire

The Athlete: Greatness, Grace and the Unprecedented Life of Charlie Ward

The Life of Dad: Reflections on Fatherhood from Today's Leaders, Icons, and Legendary Dads

"Mean" Joe Greene: Built By Football

Jocks In Chief: The Ultimate Countdown Ranking the Most Athletic Presidents, from the Fight Crazy to the Spectacularly Lazy

HEART OVER HEIGHT: THE NATE ROBINSON STORY

CONTENTS

I debated including a traditional 'contents' section at the front of this book.

At first I had it in here. Then I took it out and I'll tell you why.

This book includes 90 columns ranking and counting down the 90 things that made us legendary from the '90s.

When you're doing a countdown, it's no fun finding out the order of the countdown BEFORE the countdown even starts, right?

What would be the fun in opening the book and seeing all 90 ranked things and where they sit on our countdown – and *then* reading it?

That would be the lamest rankfest ever. And we're not lame. We're awesome. We're '90s dudes.

Of course, you *could* just flip to the back of the book and read this in reverse order, old school Rick Reilly SI column style, and that's your choice. Or you could bounce around. Or you could start at 90 and read the countdown one at a time until you get to number one.

That's the way I recommend doing it. It's serendipitous. It's cool. It's exciting. You never know what's coming next:

One minute you're reading about Gary Payton and Shawn Kemp and the next we're breaking down *Jock Jams* and then who knows, maybe we're talking about Hot Pockets or *Tommy Boy* or Warren G or Barry Sanders?

However you choose to read this book, I appreciate you taking the time to do so.

You could buy any book in the world and you chose this one.

I appreciate that.

Enjoy!

'90s Forever,

Jon

#90

Bird & Jordan's McDonald's H.O.R.S.E. Commercial

L et's start with one minor thing that has bugged me since this commercial first became iconic. Although the spot is officially called *The Showdown*, most people refer to it as "the McDonald's commercial where Jordan and Bird played H.O.R.S.E."—and I even did that in the chapter title.

HOWEVER, that's not *really* what happens.

Bird doesn't challenge Jordan to a game of H.O.R.S.E. with letters or any of that. He challenges him to a game of "first person to miss loses," with the only rule being "no dunking." His exact words are: "First one to miss watches the winner eat." Jordan agrees, and they're off. There's no mention of H.O.R.S.E., no letters, no nothing.

Thank you for letting me get that off my chest. I've been holding it in for 25 years. Now, onto the commercial.

Jordan accepts the challenge, even though we all know he has access to as many Big Macs as he wants. So does Bird, for that matter, but hyper-competitive is the name of the game for both of them, and once the challenge is made, it's on. Let's also note that Bird is in full basketball gear while Jordan is rocking what can only be described as a giant Bill Cosby sweater turned into shorts and a T-shirt (which he allegedly designed himself).

When the game begins, the first three shots they make are still within the realm of possibility:

1. A classic behind-the-backboard shot, starting with Bird, then Jordan swishing it.

2. A down-on-one-knee shot from behind the three-point line.

3. A full-court jump shot from the far side of the court.

NOTE: I'm convinced they could make this, but not without a running start—definitely not like it's a 10-footer.

But after those three, the commercial leaves basketball reality and starts having some real fun.

Bird's next shot?

"Off the floor, off the scoreboard, off the backboard, no rim." At this point, Jordan has matched all of Bird's shots, but Bird has been calling all the shots so far. And then, without explanation, Jordan suddenly starts calling the shots.

Did Bird miss one?

The commercial doesn't say, but it doesn't matter.

Here's what Jordan calls next:

4. "Over the second rafter, off the floor, nothing but net."

5. Now they're outside the arena. Jordan calls: "Through the window, off the wall, nothing but net."

6. Finally, we get the iconic shot of the two standing on top of the Sears Tower, and Jordan's masterpiece: "Off the expressway, over the river, off the billboard, through the window, off the wall...nothing but net."

The game seemingly never ends, with neither Bird nor Jordan getting the Big Mac, nor do they stop to eat a Big Mac—though the hero shot of the Big Mac makes you want one, of course.

There was a follow-up commercial featuring Bird, Jordan, and a young Charles Barkley trying to join the game, with shots being taken from the Grand Canyon, outer space, and other ridiculous places. It was fun, but it didn't capture the same magic as the original, awesome commercial, which has been quoted seven million times by you and your buddies playing H.O.R.S.E. from the 90s to today, making it the perfect entry to start our book.

Now grab a ball, grab your kid or a good buddy, and call your next shot in the driveway:

"Over the car, off the tree, through the yard, nothing but net."

#89

Jennifer Capriati

There are certain athletes and entertainers whose popularity, in hindsight, can be hard to explain unless you lived it. So if you're reading this and weren't exactly the right age in the early 90s, you might be wondering, "Finkel, why the hell is Jennifer Capriati in this book?" And that's fine, because I'm 100% confident that for most guys within about five years of my age back then, the answer is obvious: we were *all* infatuated with this cute, athletic tennis phenom, who, at 13, was on the cover of our bible, *Sports Illustrated*.

If you liked tennis, yes, Capriati was a bona fide sensation, winning tournaments when she should be in middle school. But if you were a middle school boy and you liked middle school girls—she became a curious crush for a lot of us who barely followed the sport.

Sure, we knew Andre Agassi (who we'll cover later on), Pete Sampras, Jim Courier, and Michael Chang on the men's side. And we'd heard of the big names in women's tennis like Steffi Graf and Monica Seles. But they seemed old to us young dudes—even if they were only in their 20s.

Capriati, on the other hand, looked like she could be the girl sitting next to you in Miss Swenson's algebra class. She was athletic, but she didn't look like some unattainable superstar. She looked like she could be in your yearbook.

For a lot of us, she was the first female athlete whose picture went up on our walls, right alongside our favorite baseball or basketball players. And while, yes, she should be celebrated for her incredible talent at such a young age—and she went on to have a fantastic career—Jennifer Capriati was more than that. She had a *moment* with young 90s teen dudes.

Unlike other female celebrities we knew of, she didn't seem out of reach like some tanned SI swimsuit model in a bikini on a beach in Bora Bora; and she wasn't a huge pop music star we saw on MTV every day like Gwen Stefani or Paula Abdul. No, she was the girl-next-door who just happened to be great at tennis. If you were a 14- or 17-year-old boy in the early 90s, she felt like someone you might actually know—the girl down the street, the one who might even be on your bus.

She had a small window to be sure, but for a splice of 90s dudes in middle school in '90, '91 and '92, Jennifer Capriati was the sports crush that felt somehow attainable because, um, *she was our age!*

#88

Nirvana & Pearl Jam

I f the 90s made up the biggest part of your childhood, then you probably went from double digits to college with a front-row seat to a massive cultural shift in music. As you were becoming aware of pop culture, your earliest memories of legendary bands included Bon Jovi, Def Leppard, Poison, and more—guys with feathered hair, leather jackets, random arm bands and accessories, tattoos, and an all-out effort to look like a larger-than-life rockstar.

Then, everything changed with a genre and style called grunge. These new bands weren't trying to look glamorous like Jon Bon Jovi, and they definitely weren't trying to be sex symbols like Bret Michaels. They actually made it a point of pride to look like they didn't give a shit: unkempt, disheveled, and yeah, grungy.

The two bands that took this raw new style nationwide were, of course, Nirvana and Pearl Jam. For a while there, you couldn't escape grunge music even if you tried. From every corner of the country, bands like Soundgarden, Alice in Chains, and Stone Temple Pilots came onto the scene, but it was Nirvana and Pearl Jam that truly defined grunge and took it mainstream. These bands hit the stage in giant plaid shirts, baggy tees, singing about the weight of the world and early twenties angst with raw emotion and unwashed clothes.

Personally, my first favorite grunge song was Pearl Jam's "Even Flow." It became an instant pump up anthem for me; I'd listen to it before swim races on my yellow Sony Sport Walkman to get my blood (even) flowing. And every time you turned on MTV you'd see the music video or the video for Jeremy, gnashing his teeth and biting the recess lady's breast, how could we forget?

I was never a huge Nirvana fan myself, but almost everyone around me was. Close your eyes and you can see half your middle school or high school wearing a pair of jeans, a Nirvana t-shirt and a sweatshirt tied around their waste. What a look.

Every locker had Nirvana stickers. Everyone had *Nevermind* on CD. It was impossible to escape that iconic yellow Nirvana smiley face. The opening riffs of "Smells Like Teen Spirit" played on a loop at every Tower Records in existence.

And aside from the music, one appeal these dudes had was that they didn't look like rock superstars. They looked more like the group of smokers hanging around your high school parking lot; the kind of guys who talked about starting a band.

Of course, these particular guys did start bands and made incredible music and sold millions of albums, but they looked exactly the same as the long-haired kid named Ethan who said stuff like, "Kurt Cobain is a sellout" whenever he passed someone wearing a Nirvana shirt in the hallway after class.

#87

MTV's The State

While *Saturday Night Live* and *In Living Color* were the big mainstream sketch comedy shows for most adults, if you were in high school or college in the early to mid-90s, your favorite sketch comedy show—for a short but glorious period—was MTV's *The State*. If you're reading this and never quite got into *The State*, I don't know what to tell you, other than that you missed out on a pure blast of off-the-wall, goofball, high brow and lowbrow comedy (including a sketch on highbrow and lowbrow comedy).

The State didn't follow the usual rules of sketch comedy. It went right for the absurd, with skits like "Louie," where a guy's entire personality is based on his catchphrase, "I wanna dip my balls in it!" Then there was "Barry and Levon," about two oddball buddies (one of whom is obsessed with pudding). You had "The Jew, the Italian, and the Red-Headed Gay" living together in an apartment (on Avenue A)—a skit that played off sitcom tropes and would never air today. And who could forget "Doug," the self-proclaimed "rebel" who constantly told everyone, "I'm outta here!"

The State was a show you couldn't just stream or binge. There was no TiVo, no DVR, no On Demand. MTV would air episodes, and you just had to wait for new ones to pop up—hoping they'd replay your favorites along the way. If you were lucky, you memorized the lines with your friends and started dropping quotes that nobody else understood. Knowing references from *The State* was like being in a secret comedy club, a place where you could look across the room, say *"$240 worth of pudding,"* and watch someone else burst out laughing.

It's hard to overstate the weird brilliance of *The State*. For those who were in on it, the show was pure comedy gold, and it created some of the most memorable characters and catchphrases of the 90s. So, before I finish, I have just one question for you:

What are you reading, *Generation Griffey*?

"I wanna dip my baaaaallllls in it!"

#86

There's Something About Mary

A s you go through this book, you'll see a ton of classic comedies—movies that shaped an entire generation of 90s kids who grew up on humor that perfectly evolved with us. The 90s was a golden era for dudes going from preteen to high school, right as comedy itself seemed to be going through its own growing pains.

You had your goofball PG and PG-13 hits like *Dumb and Dumber, Liar Liar, Ace Ventura, Billy Madison, Wayne's World*, and *Happy Gilmore*. But you also had the edgier, R-rated comedies that pushed boundaries, and for everyone who came of age in the 90s, there was one adult comedy that stood above all others: *There's Something About Mary*.

Mary was the Farrelly Brothers' masterpiece. It had everything: a clever plot, a series of unforgettable gags, physical comedy, sharp one-liners, and hilarious performances from every actor involved. This was a movie that you and all your buddies talked about for weeks after seeing it in theaters.

And before you saw it, you heard rumors about certain scenes and couldn't wait to see them for yourself: envelope-pushing humor that you'd never seen before.

Right from the jump, when Ben Stiller gets his "frank and beans" caught in the zipper of his tuxedo and we're *shown a close-up* of what that might look like, with a bubble and everything, we know we're in for a different kind of comedy. A better kind of comedy.

Thirty years later and you don't even have to describe the scene to anyone—just saying "frank and beans"is enough to get a laugh out of a fellow 90s dude.

And then there's the "hair gel" bit, a comedy scene so improbable it's hard to believe it happened in a mainstream film, with a payoff on the damn poster. I mean, this was a real scene in a real movie in the 90s:

Mary's standing in the doorway, Ted's "hair gel" from "flogging the dolphin" is dripping from his ear, and Mary grabs it to put in her hair.

Now, have you ever been in a theater since that moment where *more* people went, "Ooohhhhh!!!!"... And then laughed moments later when they cut to Mary with her stiff hair?

I doubt it.

But the laughs didn't stop there. Stiller's character, Ted, is the ultimate unlucky everyman, going through disasters from being mistakenly arrested as a "serial killer" to being interrogated while wearing a neck brace.

Matt Dillon's character, the sleazy private investigator, whose obsession with Mary's dog Sparky ends in an epic (and highly illegal) tussle that leaves him electrocuted and the dog hilariously unhinged. And, of course, Dillon's "chompers" line and his description of Mongo with a forehead like a drive-in theater.

Chris Elliott as Dom, Ted's buddy with the raging "hives" problem, plays the weirdo friend to perfection, complete with his own creepy obsession over Mary. And then there's the classic line from Tucker,

Mary's pseudo-English "friend" who tells Ted about his supposed "architecture" career and the Estadio Olimpico.

The cast of characters is loaded with unforgettable personalities, each adding to the craziness that builds up scene by scene with a legit plot twist at the end.

There's Something About Mary stands the test of time as the 90s comedy that truly broke through. It hit the right notes for the dude crowd in every way and became the defining adult comedy of the decade. But before we move on to the next chapter, I have a quick question:

"Do you have any change? Because all I've got are these damn Nepalese coins."

#85

NHL '94

Here's a fun fact that I think a lot of guys reading this will agree with: in the mid-90s, you played far more video game hockey than hockey you watched on television or actually played on the ice. And the reason for this? One of the all-time great sports video games—NHL '94.

From the moment you hit the video ice, passing, hitting, and nailing one-timers felt like a near-perfect gaming experience. Even if you weren't a huge hockey fan or if your hometown team was terrible, this game had you hooked. The checks were satisfying; you could absolutely flatten your opponent as they crossed center ice. You could shatter the glass with a slap shot.

Everything about it—the speed, the flow—just seemed to work better than some of the more traditional NBA or NFL games at the time. Skating across the rink felt faster, sliding and cutting around defenders felt stronger, and there was nothing better than loading up a shot, holding down that button, and sending a laser toward the goal.

Plus, the teams you could choose were loaded with players who became video game legends. The Detroit Red Wings had Steve Yzerman dominating with speed and control. The Pittsburgh Penguins with Mario Lemieux and Jaromir Jagr were practically unstoppable. And then you had the Chicago Blackhawks with the unstoppable Jeremy

Roenick, who was like the Incredible Hulk on the ice—every shot he took felt like it was going in. The New York Rangers with Mark Messier and Brian Leetch were another top choice, and of course, the Los Angeles Kings with Wayne Gretzky were popular.

Nearly every guy reading this remembers the hours spent on NHL '94. Sure, you played full seasons on Madden, and you loved NBA Jam (we'll get to those later). But for a brief moment in the middle of the decade, a decent number of guys would have told you their favorite sports video game was NHL '94, even if they rarely tuned into the NHL. You know it, I know it—we all know it.

#84

A Few Good Men

If you had to pick one movie quote from the 90s, and you had to bet your life on the fact that anyone over 35 would know the quote and the movie it's from, the safest choice might be five unforgettable words:

"You can't handle the truth!"

Think about it.

There are other contenders, sure—like Tom Cruise's "You had me at hello" from *Jerry Maguire* (which we'll discuss later)—but if your life depended on a random person knowing the quote and its origin, "You can't handle the truth!" is the one.

The reasons why this line has stood the test of time are the same reasons why *A Few Good Men* is still so powerful today. It's a military drama, a courtroom showdown, and an intense one-on-one character clash all wrapped in one.

You've got Tom Cruise as Lt. Kaffee going head-to-head with Jack Nicholson as Col. Nathan Jessup, in a battle of truth versus appearance, honor versus deception. In addition to Cruise and Nicholson delivering Hall of Fame performances, you have an outstanding supporting cast: Demi Moore as JoAnne Galloway, Kevin Pollak as Lt. Weinberg, Kiefer Sutherland, J.T. Walsh, and Kevin Bacon all holding their own. Even the actors playing Marines Dawson and Downey, whose real names you never remember, leave an unforgettable mark. Downey was a badass.

The spine of the movie are the exchanges between Kaffee and Jessup, which get better every time they share a screen. Once we've established that Caffey is going to take the case and not plea bargain to put Dawson and Downey in jail for four months (even though it's nothing, just a hockey season) we're off.

And once we hit Cuba, where Kaffey askes Jessup for the transfer order, things pick up with Nicholson's second best monologue in the movie:

"You have to ask me nicely. You see, Danny, I can deal with the bullets and the bombs and the blood. I don't want money and I don't want medals. What I do want is for you to stand there in that faggoty white uniform and with your Harvard mouth extend me some fucking courtesy! You gotta ask me nicely."

So good. Absolutely shreds Kaffee here.

From that moment on, Cruise is on his heels, and the tension only builds. In the climactic courtroom scene, Kaffee decides to go all in, risking a court martial and his entire career to finally force Jessup into a corner. When he's staring down Jessup, throwing out line after line, you're hanging on every word, right up until "Did you order the Code Red?"

This final showdown is pure cinematic power. Jessup's explosive monologue in response, is one of my top five favorite of all time.

I'm going to paste the whole thing here because it's brilliant and you should read it right now:

"Son, we live in a world that has walls, and those walls have to be guarded by men with guns. Who's gonna do it? You? You, Lt. Weinberg? I have a greater responsibility than you could possibly fathom. You weep for Santiago and you curse the Marines. You have that luxury. You

have the luxury of not knowing what I know; that Santiago's death, while tragic, probably saved lives. And my existence, while grotesque and incomprehensible to you, saves lives. You don't want the truth because deep down in places you don't talk about at parties, you want me on that wall. You need me on that wall. We use words like honor, code, loyalty. We use these words as the backbone of a life spent defending something. You use them as a punchline. I have neither the time nor the inclination to explain myself to a man who rises and sleeps under the blanket of the very freedom that I provide, and then questions the manner in which I provide it! I would rather you just said "thank you" and went on your way, Otherwise, I suggest you pick up a weapon and stand a post. Either way, I don't give a damn what you think you are entitled to!"

Incredible, right? To this day I love every word of it and have it memorized, as I'm sure many of you do, too. So many scenes. So many lines. You can't tell the story of 90s cinema without it. Oh, and don't forget: Jack is a lousy softball player.

#83

The Question

The story of how Allen Iverson ended up at Reebok is one of my favorite sports business stories of all time and I want to share it here. Not only because for a brief period of time, The Question sneaker was hotter than any pair of Jordans in the 90s, but because the story shines a line on just how big of a deal AI was his senior year at Georgetown and into the NBA.

The first thing you need to know is that while he was in college, Iverson was considered Nike's next crown prince in the sneaker kingdom. Everyone knew it. He'd been rocking Nikes since he was squeezing Capri Suns and smashing Fruit-by-the-Foot in his lunchbox days. His high school, Bethel, was a Nike school. The summer camps he attended? Nike-run. And Georgetown? A Nike shrine, complete with head coach and Nike board member John Thompson, who had Phil Knight on speed dial. You didn't need to be a Carmen San Diego detective to crack the case of Iverson's next sneaker move.

But then, in 1996, a few wild-card upstarts at Reebok dared to dream differently. They saw Iverson not just as another player to sign but as a player to build a brand around. This seed of an idea really took root when Iverson dropped that NCAA tourney dunk on Marcus Camby that seemed to say, "Yeah, I'm here to stay." Que Gaskins, who was on his way to becoming the Global VP of Reebok, saw that dunk and thought, "We gotta get this kid!" Meanwhile, his colleague Todd Krinsky had the same lightbulb moment. "That play on Camby was Iverson's calling card," Krinsky said later. It was like they'd just watched the birth of a new sneaker icon, and Reebok wanted in before Nike swooped down.

At the time, Nike had the 90s sneaker Mount Rushmore nearly filled: the Jordan line was untouchable, the Air Penny was buzzing, and with Pippen and Barkley joining the fold, Nike had the hardwoods wrapped up. FILA had Grant Hill trying to hold court. Reebok? They had Shaq and Shawn Kemp, but their kicks hadn't yet reached that magical place where sneakers became more than footwear. Reebok needed Iverson's swagger, that "lightning in a bottle," as Krinsky put it, to compete. And they were ready to bet big on him. They just had to get the old guard at Reebok on board, including CEO Paul Fireman. After some convincing, Fireman gave the green light, saying, "All right, let's do it!"

The plan was simple but genius:

Nike had a whole empire of stars, and Iverson would just be one more swoosh in their roster, but at Reebok, Iverson would be THE GUY. David Falk, Iverson's agent, laid it out: "Reebok needed a superstar, and I told them that Allen wanted his own shoe and a serious promotional push." Gaskins and Krinsky were already there. They told Iverson they'd make him the face of Reebok, showed him the early version of *The Question*, and promised it'd be ready for his first NBA game. And then, the kicker—they wouldn't try to reshape his image. No polishing, no corporate-speak, just Iverson, raw and real. Oh, and a fat paycheck.

"All along, Reebok told me they didn't want to change me," Iverson later recalled. "They just wanted me to be me."

And that was enough.

Within a few years Iverson made the entire NBA in his image: fashion, attitude, tats, stats, chains, hair and more. The Question became the symbol for all of it; a shoe for young 90s dudes who were now "over" Jordan and onto the next big (little) thing.

#82

Reservoir Dogs

"*A* *re you gonna bark all day, little doggy, or are you gonna bite?"*

The moment you finished reading that line, you probably thought of Mr. Blonde, played by Michael Madsen in *Reservoir Dogs*. And as soon as you think of Mr. Blonde, you can't help but remember the rest of the crew: Mr. White (Harvey Keitel), Mr. Orange (Tim Roth), Mr. Pink (Steve Buscemi), Mr. Brown (Quentin Tarantino), and Mr. Blue (Edward Bunker). Throw in Nice Guy Eddie (Chris Penn) and Joe Cabot (Lawrence Tierney), and you're instantly transported back to a time when you sat down to watch a truly original movie. The premise of *Reservoir Dogs*—a bank robbery gone wrong—wasn't unique, but the execution? Flawless.

It's hard to overstate the impact *Reservoir Dogs* had on 90s dudes. The dialogue crackled with tension and humor. The ball-busting banter between the characters was unreal. And the concept of using color-coded names for each character? Genius. The movie was also an endless quote-fest, with lines that you'd hear repeated over and over again:

"Let's go to work."

"I don't tip."

"You shoot me in a dream, you better wake up and apologize."

Aside from making it cool to have endless conversations about the minutiae of pop culture, when you tear away the plot, *Reservoir Dogs* is about a bunch of guys being dudes living outside normal society, with no wives or girlfriends around; going to diners, meeting in bars, doing whatever the hell they want whenever they want. Mr. Blonde and Mr. Pink and the boys were modern old west outlaws. They were tough, unpredictable and volatile – but they lived by a code. Did that mean that all of us watching this Tarantino movie wanted to be bank robbers? No. But did we want to have a crew we could shoot the shit with over breakfast for a few hours? Hell, yes.

The other important legacy of this movie is the soundtrack. I can't think of any other way that a group of fifteen-year-olds in 1993 would be buying CDs with songs like 'Stuck in the Middle of You' by Steelers Wheel and 'Hooked on a Feeling' by B.J. Thomas on them. I'd never even heard of these songs before the movie (they came out before I was born), but suddenly they were high school hits.

Side note: For years, I didn't know what the title *Reservoir Dogs* meant. It wasn't until Google came around that I learned that rats around the Los Angeles reservoir are called Reservoir Dogs, because they grow to the size of dogs. Since the entire movie revolves around trying to find the rat in the group, Quentin Tarantino's clever title made sense—and was way better than calling it *Rats*.

If you haven't seen this movie in a while, I promise you, it holds up. The dialogue is just as sharp, the tension just as palpable, and the characters just as memorable. Go ahead, don't just talk about watching it—*watch it*. Because if you don't, I have to ask: "Are you gonna bark all day, little doggy, or are you gonna bite?"

#81

Shawn Kemp & Gary Payton

The mid-90s NBA basketball universe was undeniably dominated by Michael Jordan and his return to the Bulls. But in terms of popularity, we had a few teams that crossed over into mainstream NBA fandom, away from just their local market.

In the early 90s we had the Magic and Hornets and of course later we had the Phoenix Suns with Charles Barkley joining Dan Majerle and Kevin Johnson in their Finals run. Patrick Ewing always kept the New York Knicks in the conversation, and by the late 90s, the Lakers picked up steam with Shaq and Kobe. The Utah Jazz made two Finals appearances with Karl Malone and John Stockton, but in terms of sheer popularity and pop culture crossover? The Jazz didn't quite cut it.

No.

There was only one mid-to-late 90s squad that fell in the "I love that team" category from the northwest to the northeast, and that was the 1996 Seattle SuperSonics.

First, let's talk about those green and yellow uniforms. Classic. Flashy. Exciting. The Sonics' name, born in the 70s after Seattle got the franchise, was a nod to hypersonic jets—it implied speed, power, and flight. And the team itself embodied that perfectly.

You had Gary Payton, the trash-talking, relentless point guard who locked down opponents on defense and was fearless on offense. Payton was the face of the team, always running the show (and his mouth).

Then, you had one of the top 10 dunkers of all time—and arguably one of the top two or three in-game dunkers ever—Shawn Kemp. Kemp was an unstoppable force, known for his ferocious slams, blocks, and running the wing like no one else. If you wanted to beat the Sonics, you had to stop Kemp, and good luck with that.

Rounding out the crew, you had the super versatile All-Star Detlef Schrempf, Nate McMillan as the glue guy and the brilliant George Karl as head coach. The 1996 Sonics were formidable and fun, giving Jordan and the Bulls a serious challenge in the NBA Finals. They ultimately fell to the Bulls 4-2, but to this day Karl and crew feel like they should have won that series.

In terms of teams beloved by their city—and still beloved by NBA fans today—the Sonics are at the top of the list (even though they currently don't exist).

They were larger than life, and in the NBA Jam video game, they were the perfect team. You had Payton for steals and assists, Kemp for triple flip, thunderous dunks, and Detlef Schrempf to nail those threes. For many (including yours truly), they were the go-to team in the game.

Bottom Line: those 90s Sonics were awesome. They had personality, they had style—hats, jerseys, jackets, warm-ups— they had swagger. And for East Coasters who hated the Lakers and were bored with the Jazz and who didn't care about the Blazers, they were an easy team to root for out West.

#80

Summer Sanders

The first Olympics that most 90s dudes were likely aware of was the 1992 games in Barcelona, Spain. By the time 1996 rolled around, we were probably firmly in high school, or even college. But that first Olympics for us, when we were pre-teens or early teens was the '92 games. And one of the golden girls of those games—the face of the U.S. women's Olympic swim team—was none other than Summer Sanders.

Now, I'll admit, I'm biased on this front. I'm a lifelong swimmer, and for much of the early 90s, Summer Sanders was my dream girl.

You'll understand because we had so much in common:

I was a butterfly swimmer, she was a butterfly swimmer and... um.... well... that's about where the similarities ended, but man, I had a huge crush on her.

Summer Sanders wasn't just pretty and athletic and seemingly fun to hang out with; she was dominant in the pool. She was a record-breaking swimmer at Stanford, and she went on to win two gold medals and four total medals at the '92 Olympics—including a gold in what used to be my signature event, the 200-meter butterfly. She was strong, fast, and awesome.

And since I'm the ultimate decider of who belongs in *Generation Griffey*, Summer Sanders gets the nod on her athletic achievements alone. But where she truly separates herself from other swimmers—like my other child swimming heroes Matt Biondi and Mel Stewart—is the fact that Summer crossed over into the mainstream.

After dominating the pool, Summer Sanders became a co-host of *NBA Inside Stuff* (which we talk about later in this book), on her way to becoming a full-fledged TV personality, hosting *Figure It Out* on Nickelodeon, *Inside Out* on ESPN, and making appearances on *The Sports List* and *Skating with Celebrities*. She was all over 90s television, crossing from sports into pop culture like few athletes could.

Honestly, I couldn't live with myself if Summer Sanders didn't have a chapter in *Generation Griffey*. And this puts her in rarified air. She's one of the few athletes who appears in both this book and was once on a poster in my childhood bedroom haha.

#79

The Ultimate Maniacs

L ate 1980s WWF wrestling was dominated by a cast of larger-than-life superstars: Hulk Hogan, Macho Man Randy Savage, Ricky "The Dragon" Steamboat, Junkyard Dog, Jake "The Snake"
Roberts, and so many more. But undeniably, the 80s belonged to
Hulk Hogan. He was the face of wrestling—*the* icon. Sure, Macho
Man had his moments of superstardom, but it was Hogan's larger-than-life persona that dominated the decade.

But by the early 90s—1990, 1991—something shifted. While
Hogan was still the A-lister, for many, the true favorite was Macho
Man Randy Savage. And then, like a gift from the wrestling gods, The
Ultimate Warrior exploded onto the scene.

The Ultimate Warrior was a force of nature. He was more muscular
and more massive than both Hogan and Macho Man. With his body-
builder physique, warpaint, wild, flowing hair, and warrior strings tied
around his bulging arms, he looked like his muscles might explode at
any second.

When he sprinted full-speed from the locker room to the ring,
shaking the ropes to communicate with his "warrior gods," the crowd
went absolutely nuts. It was electric. And when he lifted giants—Hulk

Hogan included—into a gorilla press slam, it was pure adrenaline. Warrior had this supreme energy that no one could match.

And then, in 1991, something unbelievable happened—Macho and Warrior joined forces to become The Ultimate Maniacs.

The promos they cut together were pure dynamite. Macho Man, with his gravelly voice, would explain what "Macho Madness" was all about while the Ultimate Warrior would channel his warrior energy, screaming into the camera like a bolt of lightning. The two of them on screen together had enough high voltage to knock out an entire town. Their tag team run was short, but while it lasted, the Ultimate Maniacs were the most electrifying duo in wrestling.

Though they eventually faced off for championship belts, for that brief moment, two of the most beloved and high-energy wrestlers—Macho Man and The Ultimate Warrior—stood side by side as tag team partners. And for fans, it was something special.

Long live *The Ultimate Maniacs* ooooohhh yeahhhh!!!!

#78

Kathy Ireland & Necessary Roughness

If we were taking bets on the first swimsuit model who comes to mind for 90s guys, I'd put my money on Kathy Ireland. She had a unique ability to embody both the supermodel and the girl-next-door qualities in a way that made her stand out. She wasn't statuesque like "The Body" Elle Macpherson, or instantly striking like Tyra Banks, or a classic blonde bombshell like Rachel Hunter or Christie Brinkley.

Yes, Ireland was absolutely supermodel-level beautiful, but she also had a certain cuteness that made her feel more relatable, like she could've been the homecoming queen at your local high school. That was part of her appeal.

The other part? She appeared in one of the greatest undercover sports movie cult classics of the 90s: *Necessary Roughness*. As a kicker.

Truth be told, Kathy Ireland in her cutoff gray Texas State shirt is a signature image of the decade. That movie solidified her status with sports-loving, supermodel-appreciating dudes everywhere. No other supermodel managed to pull off this unique combo—gracing the cover of the *Sports Illustrated Swimsuit Issue*, appearing in it 13 straight times, and being a star in a sports movie that had undercover staying power.

While other models were dazzling on magazine covers, Kathy managed to make the jump into sports and pop culture in a way that made her feel both glamorous and down-to-earth.

And here's an interesting thing to keep in mind:

Kathy Ireland is now worth about a half-billion dollars! Her licensing company brings in over 3 billion dollars a year and has over 17,000 products. Not bad for the former kicker of the Armadillos.

As for the Texas State Armadillos themselves? Man, we really got ourselves a random cast for this one:

Robert Loggia and Hector Elizondo as coaches.

Scott Bakula as the washed up QB making a comeback.

Larry Miller as the dean. Sinbad as an ex-high school star. And even Lattimer & Alvin Mack from *The Program* (don't worry, we get to that later).

To top things off, there's a scrimmage against a team of "convicts" played by a group of NFL stars including Jerry Rice, Roger Craig, Earl Campbell, Dick Butkus, Tony Dorsett, Too Tall Jones, Jim Kelly, Randy White and Herschel Walker.

Add it up and this is a football movie that won't be mentioned among the greatest sports films of all time – but that does earn a mention in *Generation Griffey* because when you're in the closing seconds of a football game and you've given it your all trying to win, never forget these words of wisdom by Paul Blake:

"You're hurt. You're tired. You're bleeding. I'm gonna make you a promise. We get into that end zone, you're not gonna feel any pain."

#77

The Annoying Mentos Freshmaker Commercial

I debated whether to include this commercial in the book about a dozen times. My first thought? This might be the most annoying commercial for dudes who grew up in the 90s—of all time. My second thought? It's a commercial for Mentos. Nobody actually eats Mentos, so why include it in a book like this? But then, after watching the commercial again, I realized something: the commercial itself, in addition to its unforgettable jingle, is so completely and utterly 90s that it *had* to be included.

I know you remember the song, so I won't even pretend that some of you don't:

"Mentos, fresh and full of life!"

It's a Hall of Fame jingle that sticks in your head forever. But the commercial? The premise is about this kid—dressed in peak 90s fashion, with floppy hair, oversized clothes, and sneakers—hanging out at a classic old school mall. The whole commercial revolves around this dork trying to avoid being stuck with his mom - something we can all relate to.

The pack of Mentos becomes his secret weapon. He holds it weirdly in a thumbs-up position the entire commercial, like it's some magical artifact. He's constantly ditching his mom, using the "power" of Mentos to evade her. At one point, he even pretends to be a mannequin in a store window, complete with frozen pose, while his mom walks right by him. Then, in the grand finale, she gets stuck on the down escalator while he's triumphantly on the second level. The freshmaker strikes again.

It was goofy. It was silly. And it was everything you loved about 90s commercials. Long before we had the ability to fast-forward through ads, before TiVo, YouTube TV, or streaming, if you were watching TV—especially Saturday morning TV—this Mentos commercial was on at least 437 times in the span of a few hours. There was no escaping it. You watched it so many times that you could probably still recite every beat, and by the end of the morning, you'd be walking around humming the jingle to yourself: "Mentos, the freshmaker!"

It didn't matter that the plot was ridiculous, or that nobody you knew actually bought Mentos.

And now I have to apologize to you, because you're probably singing it in your head: *Mentos fresh and full of life... Mentos, the freshmaker!*

#76

Speed

O
f all the impending disaster action movies we've ever
had—where there's a ticking clock from start to finish—*Speed*
stands out with one of the best premises ever. A madman takes control
of a city bus, and if it goes below 50 mph, it blows up. Simple, right?
But that setup instantly makes you curious and floods your brain with
questions.

How long can you really keep a bus going over 50 mph in a city?
How much gas is in the tank, and how long can it last? And, of course,
how is the speed being monitored?

Thankfully, the man who navigates us through these stressful
questions and saves the day is none other than Keanu Reeves. This is
classic action movie Keanu—stoic, determined and affable as LAPD
Officer Jack Traven, the hero who's going to keep those bus riders safe.
Speed might not have the over-the-top special effects of some of our
other favorite 90s action flicks, but it makes up for it with relentless,
high-stakes action and holy-shit level suspense.

The movie opens with a nail-biting elevator rescue, setting the
stage for what's to come. We've got a mad bomber, Dennis Hopper,
cranking up the tension as the villain with a personal vendetta. We've
got Jeff Daniels as Keanu's partner, adding some balance and humor,

especially in their earlier scenes where they disarm a bomb on a moving elevator.

But at the heart of the movie?

It's all about Jack and Sandra Bullock's character, Annie, the accidental heroine who suddenly finds herself in the driver's seat—literally.

On a personal fun note, I remember rewatching this movie with some friends when I moved to Los Angeles a long time ago and it spawned a great theoretical statistics question:

Assuming that you were Jack and that the events in *Speed* really happened, meaning, there was a bomb on a bus and you hopped on to help.... What would be the legitimate odds that there would be a young, attractive girl stuck driving the bus after the driver was shot?

A thousand to one? Ten thousand to one? Have you ever been on an LA city bus? I'd ride them occasionally when I lived out there and I can assure you that this was not typically the mode of transportation in Hollywood for A-List looking actresses haha.

I think you'd probably have a greater shot of hopping on a bus with an actual bomb strapped to it than of hopping on and seeing someone like Sandra Bullock or Halle Berry driving.

Now back to the column:

From the moment the bus hits 50 mph and the bomb arms itself, the action is relentless. You've got buses jumping over freeway gaps. You've got civilians jumping from the bus into speeding cars. And there's that incredible scene when Jack slides under the bus on a dolly to defuse the bomb, only to realize there's a second trigger. It's edge-of-your-seat stuff from beginning to end.

Close your eyes, and you can practically hear the roar of the bus engine, the screeching tires as they make hairpin turns in the L.A. traffic, and the gasps of passengers as they narrowly avoid disaster at every turn. You even probably remember that goofy cameo by Cameron from *Ferris Bueller's Day Off*. The whole thing culminates in a subway chase with Jack and Annie trying to stop yet another bomb—because, apparently, the bus just wasn't enough chaos for one day.

And like all iconic action flicks, *Speed* leaves you with a line that sticks. Dennis Hopper's challenge is unforgettable: "Pop quiz, hot-shot." That's the moment you knew you were in for a ride. *Speed* has everything you want. High-stakes action, a brilliant/crazy villain, impossible scenarios, and a ticking clock that keeps you glued to your seat. And it gave everyone some great life advice:

If you're ever in a situation where you're pointing a gun at a bad guy who is threatening to kill his hostage: shoot the hostage. Take them out of the equation.

#75

The Simpsons

Yes, I know *The Simpsons* are still on the air. And yes, I know they're probably just as good in Season 48 or whatever as they were in their early years. But without offending the die-hard Simpson super fans, I think it's fair to say that the true heyday of the show was in the early to mid-90s. I write this because while *The Simpsons* continues to air new shows, their cultural impact today is a mere fraction of what it was back when they burst onto the scene.

In the 90s, *The Simpsons* were a cultural juggernaut. You couldn't walk through a mall or a middle school without seeing at least a dozen kids rocking Bart Simpson T-shirts. And it wasn't just Bart—Marge, Homer, Lisa, even Maggie—they were everywhere. There were Simpsons toys, lunchboxes, posters. Personally, I had a Bart Simpson poster in my locker in fourth or fifth grade.

At that age, we weren't old enough to appreciate Homer's subtle takes on society or catch the clever jabs at pop culture written by the ex-Harvard Lampoon writers. We were too young to care about satire. But we *did* care that Bart didn't listen to his parents, skated around town, got into trouble, and mostly got away with it. He was the coolest troublemaker on TV.

We loved it when Bart said, "Eat my shorts." We loved it when he dropped "Don't have a cow, man." And "Cowabunga, dude!"—you couldn't walk down the hallway at school without hearing someone say one of those three. In fact, the shirt I personally owned proudly displayed the classic "Eat my shorts" line. It was hard to be a little dude in the early 90s and not be a Bart Simpson fan.

And it wasn't just about the show. There was even a surprisingly fun Simpsons video game, where Bart skated around, hitting people with his skateboard, and Marge would whack enemies with a vacuum cleaner. That's how big The Simpsons were—they had an entire video game built around their cartoon characters, none of whom were superheroes, and it was awesome.

So, while some fans might argue that *The Simpsons* is just as funny today as it was back then, I can say firsthand I have no idea. I haven't watched in twenty years. Maybe it still is clever, maybe it's not, but it's hard to capture the same magic that defined the early 90s. Back then, *The Simpsons* weren't just a half-hour slot on Sunday night—they were a phenomenon.

And to anyone who disagrees... Don't have a cow, man.

#74

NBA Inside Stuff

G rowing up as a hoops fan in the 90s—whether you were in fifth
grade, eighth grade, or even early in high school—there was no
real way to get to know your favorite NBA players beyond the court.
Sure, you could follow the local newspapers and maybe catch a few
nuggets about them, but you weren't getting any insight into their
personal lives. You never saw their homes, their cars, or heard them talk
about what food they liked, the music they listened to, or the movies
they were into. That kind of access didn't exist.

If you were lucky, you might get a profile in *Sports Illustrated for
Kids*, or see your favorite player make the cover of *Sports Illustrated*.
But even then, you were just getting a glimpse—a few quotes, maybe
a cool story about their high school days or a quirky pregame ritual.
But real personality? That was hard to come by.

Enter *NBA Inside Stuff*.

Hosted by Ahmad Rashad, *NBA Inside Stuff* was like an Instagram
story before Instagram existed. Every Saturday morning, you'd tune in
to get an insider look at the lives of your favorite NBA stars. Ahmad
was as excited to talk to these guys as you were to hear from them.
Sure, they talked hoops, but the beauty of the show was that it often
took you beyond the game. Ahmad would visit players at their homes,
give you a tour of their crib, and maybe even shoot around in their

driveway. You'd see them with their families, hear about the charities they were involved in, or learn about the music they were bumping in their cars.

The guest list read like a Hall of Fame roll call.

You'd see Michael Jordan showing off his golf swing, Charles Barkley cracking jokes and giving fans a glimpse of his off-court persona, and Shaquille O'Neal being, well, Shaq—goofing off, doing impressions, and giving tours of his massive rides. Grant Hill might play a little piano, or you'd catch Reggie Miller taking you behind the scenes of one of his epic three-point contests. They'd show Hakeem Olajuwon at a local charity event, or take you inside Patrick Ewing's home as he hung out with his kids.

It wasn't just about stats or highlights—it was about the stories. You'd see Gary Payton and Shawn Kemp having fun off the court, joking around like they were still in the Sonics locker room. You'd watch David Robinson and learn about his Navy background, or see Dikembe Mutombo giving back to his community. Ahmad made sure we saw the "real" side of players like Scottie Pippen, Chris Webber, and Tim Hardaway, too.

Ahmad Rashad was like a bridge between us and the NBA superstars we admired. He had this unique ability to connect with the players, and you could tell they felt comfortable with him. And that meant we, as fans, got to see the human side of our idols, the side that wasn't always visible during a game. So here's a big shout out to *my man* Ahmad for making it happen for us 90s dudes.

#73

Atlanta Braves Pitching Staff

I t's been thirty years and right now you can name most of the starting rotation for the 1995 Atlanta Braves, even though most of you don't live in Atlanta and didn't care that much about the Braves growing up: Greg Maddux, Tom Glavine, John Smoltz. Steve Avery.

Done. Done. Done. Done.

Is there any other baseball team you can do this with besides your favorite team growing up? In fact, can you even do this with your favorite team growing up? It's always easy to remember an ace or two, but the third and fourth starters? From thirty years ago? C'mon.

And yet...

Just about any 90s baseball fan can for sure knock out Maddux, Glavine & Smoltz when you ask, "Name me the top of the Braves starting rotation in the 90s."

Can you do that for the Red Sox? The Yankees? The Dodgers?

Unless you were a Sox, Yanks or Dodgers fan, probably not.

Yeah, in the late 90s and early 2000s you'll get Pedro and Schilling and Pettitte and Clemens easy, but that might be it. Or maybe you'll remember Schilling and Randy Johnson in Arizona. Who knows?

The point here is that it's beyond rare to remember four starters on a team you barely followed... But here's the catch: TBS.

You may not have specifically *wanted* to follow the Braves back in the day, but they were on TV *all the time* because they were owned by Ted Turner and he aired their games nationally on his network.

Add in the fact that from 1991 to 1998 Maddux, Glavine and Smoltz accounted for seven of the eight Cy Young Awards in the National League and you can understand why we all had these dudes imprinted on our hard drives.

One thing I didn't remember is that Maddux actually won his first Cy Young in 1992 with the Cubs, then won in '93 with the Braves in the middle of winning four in a row. Regardless, you can't talk 90s baseball without bringing up the Braves starting pitching – an anomaly of dominance that still holds up three decades later.

#72

Florida State Football

I f the swagger of "The U" defined 1980s college football, then the garnet and gold of Bobby Bowden's Florida State Seminoles defined the 90s. Year in and year out, the road to the national championship ran through Tallahassee. Florida State was either undefeated or *damn close* every year, and they spent the better part of the decade in the top five or top ten.

You want stats? How's this:

The 1990s Florida State Seminoles had the most wins by a football team in a decade. Ever. They were 109-13-1 over the course of 10 years. That's an insane 89% winning percentage, with two national championship to show for it in '93 and '99.

FSU also rolled out one iconic player after another, and they were known for two things: athleticism and swagger. Sure, they had Deion Sanders in the 80s, but in the 90s?

The teams were loaded with all-world talent.

Charlie Ward was one of the biggest names in college football, winning the Heisman Trophy, leading FSU to a national championship in 1993, and then doing the unthinkable—going to the NBA and becoming a starting point guard for the New York Knicks in the NBA Finals.

But Charlie Ward wasn't alone. Florida State was stacked. You had Warrick Dunn, who ran through defenses like a speedy wrecking ball, eventually becoming a Pro Bowl running back in the NFL. You had Peter Warrick, one of the most electrifying wide receivers and punt returners in the game at the time.

And let's not forget the defense—Derrick Brooks was a beast who would go on to have a Hall of Fame career in the NFL and who anchored the Seminoles' defense in the early 90s. Then there was Sam Cowart, a hard-hitting linebacker, and Terrell Buckley, a shutdown corner and return man who won the Jim Thorpe Award and went on to be a first-round NFL pick. You could throw in Corey Simon, a dominant defensive tackle, and Javon Walker, who would also make his mark in the NFL.

Florida State was a factory for future NFL stars. They were so fast and so dominant that they earned the nickname "Free Shoes University" during a recruiting scandal that only added to their lore. These guys were everywhere—Sports Illustrated covers, highlight reels, you name it.

And then there was the top-to-bottom cockiness, giving the Seminoles such an outsized style that the movie *The Program* was rumored to be based on Florida State's football culture. Every Saturday, FSU was must-see TV.

Yes, the 90s were packed with great teams—Steve Spurrier and his Fun 'N Gun Florida Gators had dominant moments, and Nebraska with Tommy Frazier seemed invincible at times. But year in and year out, Florida State was always right there, contending for national championships - and letting everyone know about it.

#71

New Jack City

I'm willing to bet that almost everyone reading this saw *New Jack City* a few years before they probably should have. You were a little too young, a little too suburban, and way too green to fully grasp what *New Jack City* was about. But still, something about it drew you in. Maybe you were 13, 15, or 16, and you found a way to see it. Maybe you snuck into the theater, or maybe you convinced your parents to rent it from Blockbuster without really telling them what it was about.

Either way, you got your hands on it.

There was so much about *New Jack City* that hooked you right from the start. Wesley Snipes as Nino Brown—this larger-than-life drug kingpin rising to power. Ice-T, playing the gritty cop determined to bring him down. And then there was Chris Rock as Pookie, the undercover crackhead you couldn't help but root for, even though you knew he'd never really escape the habit. The movie was edgy, raw, and real - as far as you knew. It gave you a hard look at the world of a drug empire, but most of us who watched it while living 50 or 100 miles from the nearest city didn't fully grasp the social commentary - we just knew it was "hard".

The soundtrack alone was enough to draw us in.

When *New Jack Hustler* dropped, you knew you had to see this movie. And once you did, you were sitting in your room, quoting it with your buddies: "Am I my brother's keeper? Yes, I am!"

The movie had everything.

The backstabbing, the betrayal, the tense chess game between Nino and the system; between Nino and his rivals; between Nino and his own crew. Who would survive? Who would win?

New Jack City was our *Scarface*. It had that same violent, cartoonish feel. The same over-the-top performances.

It was a gritty, stylish (the purple and neon outfits are so awesome), and unforgettable snapshot of the early 90s, and it left its mark on all of us, making us think about loyalty, survival, and power in a way no other movie did at the time. It also gave us this line that we could endlessly repeat every time one of our buddies interrupted us:

"Sit your five dollar ass down before I make change."

And never forget this important piece of life advice:

"Money talks, and bullshit runs a marathon. So, see ya and I wouldn't want to be ya."

#70

Wu-Tang

Before Wu-Tang was for the children, Wu-Tang was for college kids. It's a fact of higher education that roughly 65% of dorm rooms and frat house walls between 1992 and 1997 had a Wu-Tang poster proudly displayed. The music, of course, was reason number one, but it wasn't just about individual songs—it was the entire ensemble. The whole clan appealed to us. Wu-Tang wasn't just a group of rappers—they were like an early Avengers of hip-hop.

You had Method Man, Ghostface Killah, Raekwon the Chef, RZA, GZA, Inspectah Deck, U-God, Masta Killa, and of course, the wild card: Ol' Dirty Bastard. So many cool (and odd) names, so many different styles, all packed into one supercrew that you kind of wanted to hang out with: they busted on each other, they smoked a lot of weed, RZA and GZA were into chess, and they were obsessed with kung fu movies.

In fact, they spliced so many clips from old-school kung fu flicks like *Shaolin and Wu Tang* and *The 36th Chamber of Shaolin* into their albums that listening to their music felt like watching indy martial arts films. It also felt like they were letting you into their crew, sharing their inside jokes.

But we also can't understate how the packaging of Wu-Tang was just as powerful as the music. That unmistakable yellow "W" logo?

It was everywhere. It was a badge of honor, a bat symbol for anyone who was into the Wu. T-shirts, posters, CD covers—you couldn't walk across a college campus in the 90s without seeing that symbol. Wearing the Wu-Tang logo meant you were part of something bigger than yourself..

And the music? It was gritty and catchy at the same time. Tracks like "C.R.E.A.M.," "Protect Ya Neck," and "Triumph" could be listened to over and over. Wu-Tang's raw sound and unapologetic approach drew you in, and before you knew it, you were quoting kung fu films and Method Man lyrics.

The music, the symbol, the camaraderie—it all became an unforgettable part of the 90s experience. So whether you were bumping *Enter the Wu-Tang (36 Chambers)* or rocking that yellow "W" on your chest, you were part of the movement.

Wu-Tang forever.

#69

Big League Chew vs. Bubble Tape

L et's talk about gum.

When you're an adult, gum becomes utilitarian. You think about it if you need it; when your mouth is dry, if you want fresh breath before a meeting; or maybe you just gnaw on a stick out of boredom while driving.

Even worse, as an adult, the flavors you buy are boring; often some sugar-free spearmint, peppermint, icy mint, winter mint—basically, anything with "mint" in the name. Maybe you live on the wild side and go with cinnamon from time-to-time, but overall, adult gum flavors *suck*.

Back in the day, though, gum was an experience - an adventure for your mouth. We're talking about the golden age of gum—Bubblicious, with its unbeatable fake watermelon and fake grape flavors, and Hubba Bubba, which wasn't as good but still had its fans. Or even Gatorade Gum, which was delicious for 4.9 seconds before becoming a tasteless wad of cement. But even those couldn't top the kings of 90s gum.

There were two brands that stood above the rest, and it wasn't just the flavor—it was the packaging that mattered, too. The first we're going to talk about is Bubble Tape.

Bubble Tape came in a plastic canister, like a tape measure but filled with three feet of gum. You'd pull off six or eight inches at a time, maybe another little strip to share with your friends, and then throw the canister back in your backpack or your back pocket. The canister protected your gum, the texture was soft and solid, and the taste lasted longer than most others, but it wasn't the coolest.

No, the king of 90s gum—and really any generation of kids—is Big League Chew.

There's no contest. That shredded bubble gum, packed in a tin foil pouch like the ones baseball players used to keep their tobacco in, was the ultimate gum experience. You'd rip open that packet, and the smell alone would hit you—hard. Even now, Big League Chew smells like childhood. Ralph Lauren should bottle the smell and make a cologne scent called *90s*. Think about it:

You'd pull out a dusty wad of that shredded gum, and as your cheeks filled with saliva, you'd bask in an overwhelming flavor rush. It was like instant happiness in your mouth.

How much gum you took depended on your mood: a pinch, a quarter of the pouch, maybe even half. Or if you were feeling bold, you'd shove the whole thing in your mouth.

And for a few glorious minutes, you'd be chewing the greatest gum of your life. Sure, the flavor only lasted about one-third of an inning of baseball and then you'd be left with a ball of rubber in your mouth, but who cared? The joy of stuffing a fistful of chewy sugar in your mouth and jawing away happily—that feeling lasted forever.

In fact, if you want to relive a piece of your childhood, go grab a pouch of Big League Chew right now. You won't regret it.

#68

Blockbuster on Friday Night

Instead of a column for this one, I'm going to share what I call my "Blockbuster Video Nostalgia Manifesto". Enjoy:

The thing our kids are missing out on with streaming movies today is the anticipation—and what I like to call the *Bold Choice*.

And to understand that, let's talk about *movie rental anticipation* first.

Fellas, you know exactly what I'm talking about here. It's that mid-90s Friday afternoon feeling: you're home from school, grabbing your friends, and heading to Blockbuster. Maybe you're even planning to sneak an R-rated movie past your parents. The possibilities were endless.

You kind of knew what movies might be out, but the truth was, you never really knew what the new releases were going to be. You'd roll into Blockbuster, cruise the New Release wall, and—without fail—there was always a surprise waiting for you. Maybe it was a movie you missed in the theater, or a film you never even knew existed. Either way, seeing something unexpected got your heart racing. You couldn't wait to grab it.

But let's not forget the veteran move: sometimes the movie you wanted was all rented out. That's when you'd casually check the return pile, and *BAM*—there it was, like buried treasure, still warm from the previous rental. Pure victory.

And then, you had exactly 48 hours to watch that movie before it had to be returned. That little blue and yellow tape became the center of your weekend. It was a mini-event. There was no "I'll watch it whenever"—you had a deadline. The stakes were high.

Now, onto the *Bold Choice*.

Modern streaming is like a buffet of mediocrity. You can start watching something, hate it, switch to something else, and repeat the process without consequence. You're never penalized for picking a dud. There are endless options at your fingertips, and you never have to commit.

But back in the day, Blockbuster made you commit. You had to make a *Bold Choice*. What one or two movies were you going to roll with for the weekend? If you missed, you were stuck with it. And your parents? They weren't driving you back just because you thought "*Stop! Or My Mom Will Shoot*" was terrible. Oh no, you were in for the long haul.

The VHS or DVD cover mattered. The description mattered. The stars mattered. You had to go with your gut, make your choice, and live with it. Once you walked out of Blockbuster, that was it. You paid for your decision. Now came the anticipation: would the movie be as good as you hoped?

Streaming has ruined all that. Sure, there's no going back, but man, I'd love to take my kids to Blockbuster just once. Make them browse the aisles. Make them choose. And I'm 100% confident they'd love it, too.

#67

Air Max '94

We cover a lot of baseball shoes in this book, but when it comes to everyday wear, there was one shoe that stood out—the Nike Air Max '94. This was the shoe you wanted, your friends wanted, and even your dad wanted. Why? The giant air pocket in the heel.

Back in the day, when little things mattered—like having the right Champion sweatshirt or Umbro shorts—your shoes were a statement. And if your everyday kicks didn't have a visible air bubble below your ankle, well, you were out. The Air Max '94 was like a badge of coolness that came with a placebo effect: it made you feel faster and more athletic; like you could run a little harder or jump a little higher.

The Air Max '94 came in some basic colorways, but also some bolder ones that really popped. But what made it so popular was its versatility. If you were a kid in the 90s, the Air Max 94 was the ultimate all-purpose shoe. It was perfect for a game of kickball or touch football at recess. You could wear it for soccer, basketball, and of course, running. It didn't matter what sport you were playing or what activity you had planned—the Air Max '94 had your back.

And even today, there's nothing quite like slipping on a comfortable pair of these legends. And here's another bonus: if you were on the shorter side growing up, these shoes were sneaky, too, giving you a nice little inch boost compared to basic sneakers like Converse or Reebok. That extra lift mattered.

In the 90s, flashy shoes served multiple purposes. They weren't just for showing off—they were functional. And there was a good chance that half the kids in your school were rocking a pair of Air Max '94s at some point. Whether you were sprinting across the field or just cruising through the hallways, those shoes were a staple in the 90s wardrobe.

#66

Tombstone

O ne thing you need to know before you read this column is that I minored in English in college and wrote my final thesis on *Tombstone*.

Yes, this is a verifiable fact. Even better? I got an A-.

Tombstone is badass for so many reasons. It's got killer dialogue, legendary characters, and one of the greatest acting performances of all time—Val Kilmer's Doc Holliday. It's got good versus evil, action-packed standoffs, dudes having each others backs and more, checking all the boxes for things we love. And, of course, it's a Western, another thing we love.

When I wrote my thesis, I focused on one central theme: brotherhood.

The brotherhood in *Tombstone* is why men are drawn to it. Sure, the gunfights and the one-liners are legendary, but the deeper bond between these men is what makes it so special.

Yes, now that you've watched *Tombstone* for the 300th time, you're tuning in for the epic gunslinging and to hear Val Kilmer drop his "I'm your huckleberry" line (or huckle-bearer or whatever the dorks say).

You're watching it to see the tense standoff between Doc Holliday and Johnny Ringo. You're watching Kurt Russell stare down an outlaw (an early Billy Bob Thornton) and say, "Skin that smoke wagon and see what happens." Those macho moments are pure cinematic gold.

But the first time you watched *Tombstone*, you weren't hooked solely by the guns and the quotes; it was the bond between the brothers—Wyatt, Virgil, and Morgan Earp—with Doc Holliday at their side, facing down the chaos of the Wild West. The brotherhood between these men is the heart of the movie. You've got the good guys, the Earp brothers and Doc, facing off against the bad guys, Curly Bill and Johnny Ringo and the Cowboys with their red sashes.

It's a classic storytelling theme, but it's the loyalty, the friendship, and the unshakable trust between the Earps and Holliday that elevates it.

Some of the most powerful scenes in the film are the simplest: There's that famous shot of Wyatt, Morgan, Virgil and Doc walking toward the O.K. Corral, guns at their sides, ready to throw down. And after they finish the job? They're walking back through town, fire and destruction behind them, and they don't even have to say a word. They're a brotherhood, forged in blood and battle.

We watch *Tombstone* because we want to believe we'd be Wyatt Earp—rolling into town with a reputation that precedes us, and leaving as the hero. We believe, deep down, that if we were in that position, we'd have our brothers' backs to the end—just like Wyatt, Virgil, and Morgan had Doc's. And if you doubt our resolve, we'd love to shout an all-time threatening line like this:

"So run you cur. And tell the other curs the law is coming. **You tell 'em I'm coming! And Hell's coming with me you hear! Hell's coming with me!"**

#65

Tyra Banks & the SI Swimsuit Issue

Y ou can't talk about this decade without pausing for a moment to appreciate the supermodel at the apex of late 90s dude culture: Tyra Banks.

Not that there are official stats to these things, but Banks earning a coveted *Sports Illustrated Swimsuit Issue* cover in back-to-back years ('96 & '97) is like winning the Supermodel MVP award for consecutive seasons.

In a world before Instagram, where supermodels didn't post daily bikini shots and behind-the-scenes videos, the *SI Swimsuit* Issue was a gift from the dude gods; a once-a-year winter miracle.

For 13, 15, or 18-year-old dudes in the 90s, the arrival of this magazine was an event and the anticipation was a real thing we talked about. If you grew up in the northeast or midwest, it always arrived at the coldest, most miserable time of the year when summer felt like it was never coming back – late January or early February. You'd be shivering your way home from school, wearing your oversized hoodie, your face frozen, your mood low. And then, like magic, you'd open your mailbox to find the ultimate treasure: the *Sports Illustrated* Swimsuit Issue. Beaches. Beautiful women. The sun. The ocean. It was a beacon of hope, a reminder that blue skies and warmth would eventually return.

Sure, there had been plenty of iconic *SI* covers growing up. Elle MacPherson, Christie Brinkley, Claudia Schiffer—they were all legends. But when Tyra Banks landed her first cover in '97, she seemed to jump off the page. Then, the famous cover sat on the coffee table of dorm rooms and frat houses and apartments for almost a full twelve months until the new issue came out because she looked...perfect. And you don't just throw away perfection.

And then she was everywhere: Victoria's Secret. MTV. TV. Movies. She'd be on the sideline of NBA games. Wherever hot 90s people seemed to hang out, Tyra was there, reigning supreme, as she should.

#64

Swingers

A t its heart, *Swingers* is the ultimate romance movie—but not in the way you think. It's a love story between Mikey and Trent. Mikey is the soft-spoken, soulful, sensitive guy, while Trent is the loud, outgoing, charismatic life of the party. He's the ladies' man, the dude who can talk to anyone, anywhere, anytime. Every guy watching this movie—whether they were in high school, college, or in their early 20s—related to Mikey and secretly wanted to be Trent —tall, good-looking, at ease with everyone, the ultimate dude's dude.

Now throw in their friend Sue and the rest of the crew, and you've got a relatable group of guys just trying to make it in LA: navigating Hollywood parties, chasing acting roles, dealing with rejection, and most importantly, trying to pick each other up when shit's not working out.

Swingers is a coming-of-age story for an entire generation of guys. It resonated with dudes in high school and college because it felt so real. These guys were coping with failure, figuring out relationships, and trying to balance their desire for a serious connection with the freedom of being single. Mikey and Trent were stand-ins for us.

I can personally speak to the impact of this movie. I moved out to LA in 2000, several years after *Swingers* came out, but by then, the movie had achieved cult classic status. It wasn't a big hit in theaters, but thanks to DVD sales and endless cable reruns, it became a pop culture phenomenon.

Every one of my friends who visited me in LA wanted to do the "Swingers Tour"—the Derby, the Dresden etc...

The funny part? These weren't the cool bars. Local young guys in LA didn't hang out there (it was an inside joke by Favreau, apparently). But my friends insisted, and we'd listen to the soundtrack and have a few drinks and it was always a good time, and in this way, *Swingers* captured that unique time period for us.

Over the course of 96 minutes we got the full young adult 90s dude experience: sitting around with your buddies, ordering takeout, hitting on women, playing video games, talking trash, and trying to make sense of your place in the world. It was about getting digits, navigating awkward conversations, and living in that limbo between immaturity and adulthood.

And let's not forget the quotability.

"You're so money, and you don't even know it."

"You're like this bear man! With these claws!"

"Beautiful babies."

And of course:

"Vegas, baby."

#63

Dan Cortese & Bill Bellamy

I f MTV was the pinnacle of 90s pop culture, then the two dudes every guy watching wanted to be were Dan Cortese and Bill Bellamy. Few of us aspired to be the serious music news guy like Kurt Loder, and most of us didn't have much interest in hanging out with screaming teen girls and hosting *TRL* like Carson Daly.

No, what we wanted was to do the fun stuff—play in the Rock N' Jock games, host the spring break parties, and live the ultimate MTV life. And the two guys living that dream were Cortese and Bellamy.

They were young, charismatic, athletic, funny, and they played the part of the coolest dude from your high school who somehow graduated to being the party guy on MTV.

They weren't just hanging out in some studio asking musicians about their inspiration; they were out there, hosting the biggest events, partying with the hottest stars, and being at the center of all things cool. Bill Bellamy hosted *MTV Jamz* and *MTV Beach House*, while Dan Cortese was all over *MTV Sports* and hosted *MTV Rock N' Jock*, making them the faces of the network's most appealing shows to young guys.

They were the captains of the Rock N' Jock softball and basketball games, mixing it up with athletes and musicians, living out what every guy watching at home wanted to do. They were the VIPs at every MTV event—the Music Awards, the Movie Awards—you name it. They had access and the ultimate backstage pass to the best parties, and they brought us along for the ride.

It's hard to overstate just how much they embodied the wish fulfillment of every 90s dude watching. Ask any late teens/early 20s guy who was into pop culture and sports back then what their dream job would look like, and it was basically everything Dan and Bill were doing. Getting paid to hang out at MTV's spring break, crack jokes, play sports with your idols, and stand next to Heather Locklear? Yeah, we'd all have taken that job in a heartbeat.

Hats off to both of them for living the dream.

SIDE NOTE: As you know, Dan Cortese became such a crossover star that he scored one of the all-time great cameos on *Seinfeld,* playing Tony, the ultra-cool "Mimbo" boyfriend of Elaine. That Seinfeld appearance alone makes him a bona fide 90s icon.

#62

American Gladiators

There are real sports—football, basketball, baseball, hockey, tennis—the kind of sports that, as you get older, you realize you're not going to be great at unless you've been gifted with serious athletic talent. But then there are the contrived sports, the athletic competitions masquerading as "real" sports, where average guys could measure themselves against athletes in a way you'd never be able to in the NFL, NBA, or MLB.

Exhibit A in this genre? *American Gladiators*.

If you weren't a star athlete, but you still liked to think you had game, *American Gladiators* was your show. In fact, that was its singular beauty: it made weekend warriors and amateur athletes think, "I could do this."

The premise was simple: regular people—guys who could be your high school football teammates or the guy on your frat's intramural soccer team—competed in events against muscle-bound, juiced-up, superhero-like figures called Gladiators.

These weren't your run-of-the-mill athletes; these were dudes with names like Nitro, Turbo, and Laser, rocking fake tans and feathered hair straight out of a 90s action movie.

The brilliance of the show was that the events gave the Gladiators an edge, but not such an edge that a really athletic guy (you, maybe!) couldn't win. These mini "sports" were perfectly created for ex-college and high-school All-County selections to nod confidently as they watched, believing they could be victorious.

Whether it was running the gauntlet, surviving the obstacle courses, or trying to dunk on a Gladiator in Slam Ball, the show made it look *just* attainable enough for you to dream.

And let's not forget about the women. The female, kinda hot, kinda muscular Gladiators—with names like Zap and Ice - facing off against women who used to be the captain of the varsity lacrosse team at your high school.

It was 90s sports entertainment at its finest: no professional league, no multi-million-dollar contracts, just jacked-up dudes and athletic women, clashing in games that were part sport, part entertainment, all wrapped in spandex.

Every Saturday or Sunday morning, if you woke up early and there was nothing else on, that *American Gladiators* theme music would hit, and suddenly, your competitive juices would start flowing. You'd watch those weekend warriors take on the Gladiators, and for an hour, you'd believe that maybe, just maybe, you could take on Gemini or Titan, too. It was the ultimate 90s dream—part sports, part spectacle, and all awesome.

#61

CD Towers & Zip Cases

Y eah, you read that right. This column is about an accessory you probably didn't give a second thought to back in 1994, but it mattered—maybe more than any single thing you bought. It was a reflection of who you were, what kind of music you listened to, and, ultimately, how you wanted to be seen.

Thirty years before Spotify, Apple Music, or even iTunes, if you wanted to listen to your favorite songs, you had to buy them in physical form. First, there were giant vinyl albums, then cassette tapes (small, plastic rectangles with actual tape inside). But for us 90s kids, the main event was the CD.

Owning CDs was like wearing your music taste on your sleeve. And in the days before social media playlists, there were two ways to proudly display that taste to the world: the CD tower and the zip-up CD case.

First up, the CD tower. You know you had one. Maybe it was three feet tall, maybe five. If you were serious, you had a six-foot monster taking up half your room. This wasn't just a storage solution; it was a statement.

You'd slot your CDs into the metal racks, maybe arranging them alphabetically, maybe by genre, or, if you were chaotic (or lazy), just in the order you bought them. *Wu-Tang Clan* next to *Bon Jovi*, *Poison* chilling with *Snoop Dogg*—it didn't matter. The point was, anyone who walked into your room could see your collection and get a sense of who you were.

But there was a problem. You couldn't take that massive tower with you. CD cases were bulky, and the plastic jewel cases were a pain to open. That's where the *zip-up CD case* came in. This thing changed the game.

You had options: the smaller, stubby case that held 30 or 40 CDs, or the behemoth portfolio that resembled a three-ring binder, with slots for four CDs per page and enough pages to carry around 200 discs. It took years to fill up, and you took *pride* in it.

There was a ritual to it:

You'd pull a CD from the tower, carefully slide the disc out of the case, and place it into a slot your zip-up. Then you'd slide the zip-up case into your car's center console, or throw it into your backpack. That case was your portable music library, and it went everywhere with you.

It's hard to fathom now, in an age where your entire music collection lives on your phone, but back then, anyone who got in your car could flip through your CD case and know exactly what kind of music you were into. It was like letting someone read your diary—if your diary was filled with *Nirvana, Jay-Z, The Fugees, Pearl Jam* and the *Dave Matthews Band* and on and on.

These two accessories—the CD tower and the zip-up CD case—were key 90s essentials. They made your music life possible, and they were as much a part of who you were as your choice of sneakers or t-shirt. Sure, today it's all about playlists and streaming, but back then, those little plastic discs were everything.

#60

The Word "Word"

If 'dope' is the ultimate 90s word to describe how awesome something was (which we'll get to later), then the word 'word' is the perfect term for showing you agree with something, you *strongly* agree with something, or you're confused. It's like the Swiss Army knife of 90s vocabulary.

Simple, versatile, and useful for nearly every situation.

In its most basic form, 'word' was an innocent confirmation of something. For instance, a buddy says something you agree with, and instead of saying "OK" or "Got it," you just say, "Word."

It was the 90s equivalent of giving a nod in the conversation. But 'word' wasn't just one note—it had levels to it.

Example: if you were confused by what someone said, you could just raise the pitch at the end: "Word?" It's like you were questioning the entire premise.

Let's say a friend says, "Let's meet at the mall." You'd hit them with a solid "Word." But if they added, "We're seeing *Armageddon*... again," your response shifts to, "Word?"—as in, are we really doing this?

But that's not where it ends.

'Word' also had layers of excitement.

If you were really feeling something, you could step it up with "Word up." For example, if your buddy said, "We're going to see *Armageddon* for the second time and then hit up Sbarro," you'd reply, "Word up!"—because a few slices of Sbarro's after a movie is always a W.

There's also the classic "Oh, word?" which was a way to express surprise or interest. Imagine your 8th grade buddy invites you over for dinner, to which you reply, 'word'.

But then he casually drops, "My mom's making her famous lasagna tonight." You'd immediately hit them with an "Oh, word?!"—because famous lasagna is no joke, and now you're definitely interested.

Finally, the ultimate form of 'word' was when people said, "Word is bond." This was the unbreakable seal of agreement. You weren't just nodding along—you were locking it in.

To this day, millions of dudes (including me) will confirm something via text with those four simple letters: W.O.R.D.

Whether you're texting or talking, it's a nod to the fact that you understand each other. You're both speaking the same language, and in a way, you're giving a throwback high five to your childhood.

#59

Charlotte Hornets Starter Jacket

The Charlotte Hornets became an NBA franchise in 1988 and in a fingersnap they somehow became a cultural touchstone.

Yes, they drafted players who instantly became popular with hoops fans: Alonzo Mourning, Larry Johnson, and Muggsy Bogues.

But they played in a small city that most NBA fans—especially kids—had never been to. For many, Charlotte might as well have been in Europe next to Amsterdam. But when Zo started dominating the paint, Muggsy began weaving in and out of defenses, and LJ started ripping down dunks, something magical happened: the Hornets became *cool*. And the thing that tied it all together? Those perfect uniforms.

Aqua blue, purple, and white—the Hornets' color scheme was an instant eye-catcher. The logo, with that cartoon hornet dribbling a basketball, played whether you were in middle school, high school, or college. It didn't matter if you had never been to North Carolina; if you were a basketball fan, you wanted that gear.

In the pre-HD TV days, when screens were still those giant box sets, the Hornets jerseys stood out. They had this electric, almost hypnotic vibe, and it wasn't long before they crossed over from the court to the culture.

First, it was the Hornets T-shirts. You'd see purple and aqua tees popping up everywhere, even if the kid wearing it couldn't name a single player. Then it was the basketball shorts. And then, the ultimate crossover moment: the Charlotte Hornets Starter jacket.

The Hornets Starter jacket was a flat out status symbol. This big, puffy pullover, with the hoodie and half-zip and the Charlotte Hornet on the front became the number one sign of coolness for an entire generation of middle schoolers. If you owned one, you were basically royalty. Whether your mom ordered it from the old NBA catalog or a relative found one in a store, having that jacket was like winning the lottery. Suddenly, you were the king of your school.

How did you get it? Where did it come from? How much did it cost? These were the questions everyone asked.

And it wasn't just the Hornets. Other Starter Jackets were popular too: you had Shaq & Penny's Orlando Magic, Michael Jordan's Bulls, and, of course, the Knicks repping New York, but even looking back now, no Starter Jacket windbreaker quite had the cache of the Hornets one. It stood alone. It was bulky, loud, and awesome, just like the decade it represents.

#58

Tommy Boy

"*F*aaaat guy in a little cooooat....*"

If you know, you know.

Of all the comedies that defined the 90s, *Tommy Boy* holds a special place in the hearts of those of us who spent our middle school and high school years quoting Chris Farley and David Spade on a loop. It was the odd couple pairing nobody saw coming, but that we all needed.

The premise was simple: Tommy Callahan (played by Farley) needs to save his dad's auto parts business after his dad's sudden passing. To do that, he has to learn the ropes of sales, specifically in the new brake pad division of Callahan Auto.

Enter Richard (David Spade), the ultimate geeky, sarcastic sidekick. Together, they embark on a road trip that brings us some of the funniest slapstick comedy and most quotable lines of the decade.

Before *Tommy Boy*, the following phrases weren't even in our vocabulary:

1. *"That's gonna leave a mark."*

Every time you stubbed your toe, banged your elbow, or saw someone take a hit, this line was at the ready. It didn't matter if it was a light bump or a full-on wipeout; Farley said it best.

2. *"Brothers don't shake hands, brothers gotta hug!"*

Perfect for those awkward, half-hearted greetings where a handshake won't cut it. This line gave you the green light to embrace your friends like a big, lovable goofball.

3. *"Fat guy in a little coat..."*

If you've ever seen a dude squeeze into a jacket that's clearly two sizes too small, you've probably sung this line under your breath. Maybe you even pulled off the gag yourself to make your kids laugh 30 years later (guilty). Farley's bit was pure comedic genius, and it's been mimicked in offices, parties, and changing rooms ever since.

The magic of *Tommy Boy* was that it didn't try to be more than it was. It was a buddy comedy, a road trip movie, and a showcase for Farley's unmatched physical humor and Spade's quick wit. If one of your friends was trying to act cool around a girl, you'd probably drop, "Do you know where the weight room is?" just to mess with him. And let's not forget gems like, "Did you eat paint chips as a kid?" and "A lot of people go to college for seven years... Yeah, they're called doctors."

In the pantheon of 90s comedies, *Tommy Boy* is our generation's *Caddyshack*. It's a movie that gave us a dozen quotes to throw out whenever we needed to make a smart-ass comment, mock a friend, or just get a laugh.

To *Tommy Boy*, we say thank you—for the laughs, the quotes, the cow tipping, and the eternal image of Chris Farley ripping that little coat down the middle. Brilliant.

#57

The Chronic

Looking back on *The Chronic*'s success it's funny how so many of the commercial album sales were fueled by millions of dorky suburban teens (me) who had never been to the West Coast, the west side, Long Beach or even California.

We didn't know what a "G-thang" was.

Likewise for the hellafied gangsta lean.

Every single thing that Dr. Dre and Snoop and the Death Row crew rapped about was a completely foreign concept to middle class white kids in New Jersey or Virginia or wherever 2,500 miles away.

As a dad of young teens now, the entire era of music in hindsight makes me laugh because my parents had no idea what we were listening to. I had this very CD, with a big fat marijuana leaf on the cover, sitting in my room all the time as a fourteen-year-old and my mom had no idea what it even was.

I was listening to songs about drugs, gats, weed and doing gangsta shit, all through earbuds in my CD Discman while I was on the way to my algebra tutor.

And yet...

The music spoke to me. To us.

The Chronic just sounded...different...and awesome.

I'm not a music critic and I can't dissect its importance in music or rap overall... I'd be terrible at that.

But what I can tell you, which you already know, is that once that bassline dropped, that smooth synth kicked in, and Snoop came in with "One, two, three and to the fo' / Snoop Doggy Dogg and Dr. Dre is at the do'..."

That's it. You were hooked. From that moment on, you understood what dope music sounded like.

The Chronic made you feel cooler just having it in your CD case—like, if you could recite the intro to "Let Me Ride," you were pretty much halfway to being a G. And the album cover? Iconic.

That simple, understated photo of Dre, framed like a pack of Zig-Zags (which we didn't even know about), became a cultural touchpoint. You couldn't walk into a Sam Goody or a Tower Records without seeing a massive poster of Dre staring out at you from the window.

And let's not forget about the skits.

The "Deeez Nuuuts" intro always brought the house down—instant laughs, and something you and your friends could shout at each other across the cafeteria, even if it got you in trouble with the lunch lady.

Thirty years later, throw it on, and you'll still feel like it's 1992 all over again. The beats still slap, the rhymes still hit, and if you don't want to swing down to cherry stop and let me ride, then I'm not sure we can be friends.

#56

Pulp Fiction

L et's take a trip back to 1990. You're 11 or 12 years old, still very much a kid. You're not old enough to drive, and you're not into girls yet. You're just starting to form your little dude self, spending your weekends at sleepovers, gaming until the early hours, and obsessing over whatever shows and cable movies were on repeat at the time. High school feels close but still out of reach.

Now fast-forward to the mid-90s. You're now either in high school or college, and suddenly, you're part of a world where movies are more than "fun" - they're part of a broader culture that you live in where people reference scenes and dialogue and soundtracks. And if you were coming of age in that era, there was one movie that took over pop culture like no other: *Pulp Fiction*.

When *Pulp Fiction* hit, it was a revelation. It had everything—a bizarre, out-of-order plot, unforgettable dialogue, a boxing match, Bruce Willis packing heat, and Samuel L. Jackson as a one-man quote machine. Oh, and John Travolta, who you remembered from *Look Who's Talking* when you were still watching kids' movies. But now? Now he was back, rocking a black suit, drinking $5 milkshakes and dancing with Uma Thurman.

And the music? It was old, but new to you.

You definitely had never heard of "Son of a Preacher Man" but suddenly you knew all the words.

Pulp Fiction was the kind of movie you probably saw too young or wayyyy too young to truly understand, but you loved it anyway. And within a year, *Pulp Fiction* posters were plastered on the walls of every dorm room across America. Statistically speaking, 57% of all dude dorms had Uma Thurman lounging with that cigarette, staring down at you with that "you don't get it yet, but you will" look.

And the dialogue has stuck with us forever.

Half the dads I know have used a PG version of the "Say what again!" line on their own kids. So good: "What? Ain't no country I ever heard of! They speak English in What?"

Even as you're reading this you're probably smiling because the line is genius.

There are plenty of ways to sum up *Pulp Fiction*, but there's only one way to end this piece: by quoting the man, the myth, the legend—Samuel L. Jackson's Jules - who is quoting Ezekiel 25:17:

"The path of the righteous man is beset on all sides by the inequities of the selfish and the tyranny of evil men. Blessed is he who, in the name of charity and good will, shepherds the weak through the valley of darkness, for he is truly his brother's keeper..."

And if you grew up in the 90s, you don't even need the rest. You know exactly where it's going, and if you don't know, you better find out quickly before I lay my vengeance upon thee.

#55

Shaqnosis

There aren't too many shoes that can be called true originals from an artistic standpoint. Sure, we've seen plenty of technological advancements over the years—air pockets, pumps, specialized arches—but when it comes to pure design, most sneakers tend to borrow from each other.

Designers study the trends, figure out what's cool, and tweak the formula. But if you were around in the mid-90s and saw the *Shaqnosis* for the first time, it was a different story. Those shoes? They were inspired by Shaq, who came up with the idea for the design late one night when he couldn't sleep and saw the circular spiral graphics of the old *Twilight Zone* television show.

The *Shaqnosis* was like a mushroom trip that you wore on your feet. It had this bold, whirlpool design that made you feel like you were staring at a cartoon version of someone being hypnotized. You weren't actually under a spell, but you definitely couldn't take your eyes off them.

What made them stand out even more was that most sneakers at the time were all about speed and sleekness. Designers favored those streamlined, airplane-like looks, with lines running horizontal to the ground, making the shoe look fast even when it was standing still.

But the *Shaqnosis* flipped the script. The lines didn't suggest speed—they were all about rhythm, bounce, and movement. The design was captivating because it didn't try to mimic speed; it celebrated the power and presence of Shaq's game.

With most kids gravitating towards sneakers made for guards or small forwards (Air Jordan's, Air Penny's, The Question, Grant Hill's Filas and even Larry Johnson's Converse), Shaq's unique design put an unforgettable imprint on sneaker culture that lasts to this day, with crazy colorways and themed versions that still pop.

#54

The Word "Dope"

There are two words vying for the title of "Word of the Decade" when it comes to the 90s.

'Word' was the first word we covered. This is the next one:

Dope.

Back in the day, if you liked something, you didn't need to elaborate or explain. You just said, "That's dope." And if you're reading this, I assume you know exactly what that means—because in the 90s, 'dope' was more than a word. It was vocabulary as currency.

To break it down further, there were three levels of using the word 'dope'. Each one carried a distinct weight, depending on how much you wanted to praise something.

Level 1: "That's dope."

At this level, you're simply acknowledging that something is good. It's cool. It's solid, you like it, and it deserves a nod of approval. It's like when you first tried NFL Blitz or when the Jordan XI Concords dropped. "That's dope" was the equivalent of giving something a passing thumbs-up. No need to overdo it.

Level 2: "That's so dope."

Now we're getting somewhere. You're no longer just complimenting something; you're borderline *enthusiastic*. When you say something is *so dope*, you're moving into the realm of great and awesome.

For example, "That Arch Deluxe from McDonald's? So dope." Or, "*Broken Arrow* with John Travolta and Christian Slater? SO dope." This is the second tier of the 'dope' hierarchy, and it's where you start dropping it more emphatically.

Level 3: "That is SO FUCKING DOPE!"

This is it—the Mount Everest of 'dope'. If something reached this level, you were floored. The words "awesome" or "amazing" didn't cut it anymore. When you paired 'dope' with an expletive, like, "that is SO fucking dope!", it was your way of saying, "I literally have no higher praise to give."

It's the verbal equivalent of fireworks, whether you were talking about the new Air Max sneakers, a Friendly's Reese's Pieces Sundae, or the Hummer H1 in *The Rock*. You could even just say, "That shit is SO dope," and everyone knew you were blown away.

In the 90s, 'dope' transcended everything. From food to fashion, from music to movies, if something was 'dope', it had passed a secret "cool" test.

#53

Lil' Penny

L et me remind you of the goofiness/genius premise of the Lil' Penny commercials: Quiet and unassuming NBA star Anfernee "Penny" Hardaway plays the straight man to his alter ego, a two-foot-tall, trash-talking doll voiced by none other than Chris Rock.

The Lil' Penny commercials ran for two years and became instant classics, evolving from simple interactions between Penny and his puppet doppelgänger to co-starring Tyra Banks, and ultimately culminating in a Super Bowl ad that featured a who's-who of 90s icons.

We're talking Michael Jordan, Ken Griffey Jr., David Robinson, Tiger Woods, Barry Sanders, Stevie Wonder, Michael Johnson, and even Jonathan Lipnicki—the adorable kid from *Jerry Maguire* (the reason you know that the human head weighs eight pounds and bees and dogs smell fear).

But my personal favorite Lil' Penny spot?

It's gotta be the first one.

Close your eyes, and you can picture it:

Penny is in the Orlando Magic locker room, quietly getting ready for a game against the Timberwolves. Meanwhile, Lil' Penny is perched in Penny's locker, blasting some tunes on a miniature Walkman. Chris Rock, channeling equal parts Pookie from *New Jack City* and his stand-up routine from *Bigger and Blacker*, embodies the doll, and there's something about that high-pitched, little-brother energy that makes Lil' Penny both endearing and hilarious.

Mid-song, Lil' Penny pauses and starts peppering Big Penny with questions about the game. "What are those shoes called?" "Who are you playing?" "Work them inside and outside." It's classic backseat-driver behavior, and Big Penny is just trying to get his head in the game.

Then, as Penny heads out the door, Lil' Penny drops one of the most quotable lines from 90s commercial history:

Lil' Penny: Penny! Penny! Penny! Say hello to my man Kevin Garnett.

Big Penny (confused): Kevin Garnett?

Lil' Penny: Yeah, yeah, yeah, Garnett! We went to high school together. Tell him Lil' Penny from the science club says hello. Can you *DO* that for a brother?

Cue the fade out. Brilliant.

The thing I love most about this first commercial is how subtly smart it is. There's this moment where Big Penny, in classic big-brother mode, leans over to take off Lil' Penny's headphones so they can talk. It's the perfect touch—like, he knows Lil' Penny is going to keep running his mouth, so he indulges him, even though you can tell all Big Penny wants to do is tie his shoes and head to the court.

What made Lil' Penny great was that he was always out of the loop on Penny's basketball life, but he had total confidence in his hoops skills. In this first spot, he has no clue who the Magic are playing. In a later one, he's asking Penny about a road trip but doesn't care about the answer because he's throwing a party at Penny's house.

And the catchphrase? "Can you DO that for a brother?"—Chris Rock said he improvised it. It became a phrase every guy under thirty said when asking for a favor. Even today, you'll hear it drop in random conversations. And it all started with Lil' Penny.

#52

Duke vs. UNC

A long time ago, in a basketball galaxy far, far away—before "one-and-done" players and NIL deals, before regular international stars and the G League became the norm— men's college basketball *demanded* our attention. At the top of this hoops-hungry universe sat a rivalry that transcended the sport: Duke vs. North Carolina. These two schools, separated by a mere 9.8 miles, made up the most heated, captivating showdown in the game. If you were a fan in the 90s, you couldn't escape the pull of this rivalry.

On one side, you had the Duke Blue Devils, a team filled with players everyone loved to hate. Coached by Mike Krzyzewski—who somehow never aged in the 90s—Duke became known for winning and, well, being super annoying and irritating about it.

Christian Laettner was the king of making people's blood boil with his smirk, and Bobby Hurley's ability to make everyone on the opposing team hate him was elite. The floor slap was such a mockable move it showed up sarcastically on pick-up hoops courts nationwide.

Now throw in Grant Hill and Steve Wojciechowski and the yuppie Quin Snyder and Jeff Capel and goofs like Cherokee Parks, and you had a roster of guys who celebrated victories with tears—and kept winning, which only made them more insufferable. Year-after-year, every time Duke took the court, it felt like you were watching the evil Empire.

And then there was just about everyone's favorite college hoops school of the 90s: the UNC Tar Heels, led by Coach Dean Smith and later by Bill Guthridge, who incredibly made the Final Four in 1991, 1993, 1995, 1997, 1998 and 2000.

The Tar Heels had swagger, style, and, of course, Michael Jordan's legacy to live up to. They also had Vince Carter flying through the air like an F-16, Antawn Jamison bullying everyone in the paint, and a young Rasheed Wallace letting refs know exactly how he felt. They rocked the coolest jerseys—those iconic Carolina blues—and they had Nike backing them up, just like MJ. If you were filling out an NCAA Tournament bracket in the 90s, you were probably penciling in UNC and Duke in the Final Four without hesitation.

The rivalry wasn't just about the postseason, either. ACC battles between these two were must-watch TV. Didn't matter if it was a random Wednesday night—you knew the Dean Dome or Cameron Indoor Stadium would be electric. You knew Dickey V would be in full, "awesome baby!" mode. And for 40 minutes, you weren't watching college dudes, you were watching future NBA stars. Those battles, those moments—it's what made 90s college basketball unforgettable. It's okay to miss when all this mattered.

#51

The Jock Jams Mega Mix

When we think about the soundtrack of the 90s, it's tough to pick just one artist or song. Sure, there were some heavy hitters across genres - even some all-time greats - but if you really want to capture the essence of the decade, you need to go bigger than one song.

Now, what if I told you the definitive 90s anthem isn't even a song at all? It's actually a megamix—a perfect mashup of stadium bangers and SportsCenter sound bites that transported us to the heart of the arena. I'm talking, of course, about *Jock Jams*.

The *Jock Jams* mega mix was like throwing the entire sports experience—fans, players, commentators, the high of a last-second three-pointer, and the crushing low of a missed field goal—into a blender and turning it into one glorious 3-minute, 49-second track.

Picture the best moments of being inside a sports stadium, with a DJ spinning all your favorite pump-up jams, then cut to Dan Patrick and Chris Berman throwing out catchphrases like fastballs, and you've got *Jock Jams*.

It's hard to explain just how Jock Jams transcended normal music, but then again, not too many songs on the radio began with Michael Buffer's famous words, "Let's get ready to Ruuumbllle!"

Again, this megamix wasn't just a collection of songs; it was the energy of a packed house, the roar of the crowd, and the thrill of a Top 10 Play, all rolled into one.

In the first ten seconds you had snippets of "Whoomp, there it is," and "Get Ready for This" and "Pump up the Jam"... And shit just got more hyped and frenetic from there.

Then the compilation seamlessly blended in SportsCenter magic with Patrick's smooth delivery and Berman's iconic "He... could... go... all... the... way!!!!"

Wherever you listened, you were guaranteed to feel that adrenaline surge—whether you were watching a game or driving to school.

And the video?

Take all the song mash-ups we just mentioned and have a bunch of smokin' hot cheerleaders dancing to it.

This thing was built for 17-year-old dudes.

But here's the funny part: few people actually *owned* a full *Jock Jams* CD (any version). I knew maybe one person who had it in their CD case. It didn't matter, though. You didn't need to own it because *Jock Jams* was everywhere.

Even to this day, the second the megamix comes on and hits you right in the eardrum, you're instantly transporting you back to your mid-90s self.

#50

The Cowboys & Bandwagon Fans

It's hard to believe now after nearly thirty years of futility and Jerry Jones humiliation, but when we 90s kids grew up, the Dallas Cowboys were a nearly unbeatable juggernaut, full of superstars, stars and basically twenty-two Pro Bowlers.

They won three Super Bowls in four years, had four contenders for "Face of the Franchise" honors: Troy Aikman, Michael Irvin, Emmitt Smith and Deion Sanders.

Their stars had their own video games, appeared in commercials non-stop, represented the biggest brands, were on the cover of the biggest magazines and for a half-decade the Dallas Cowboys started every season as Super Bowl Contenders and the roster most stalked with A-List crossover stars.

The worst part of all this was that every kid whose NFL team sucked, or whose dad didn't have a team they rooted for together, became a Cowboys fan, making them the ultimate bandwagon fan base in sports rivaled only by the Yankees.

The payback for us is that currently, in 2024, the Cowboys are mostly a joke franchise, mixing in poor years with decent years and some good years where they choke in the playoffs.

But back in the day, when they were cranking out twelve and fourteen win seasons on the regular... UGH... most of their fans outside of Texas, who couldn't find Dallas on a map, were insufferable.

They were everywhere, showing up at school after every Super Bowl win, puffing their chests out like they personally handed off the ball to Emmitt Smith. It didn't matter if last season they were rooting for the 49ers or claiming to "just root for Deion"—as soon as the Cowboys started stacking Lombardi trophies, suddenly everyone was "America's Team's" biggest fan.

The Cowboys, to their credit, were awesome. Aikman threw dimes, Emmitt ran through defenders like it was Tecmo Bowl, and Irvin celebrated touchdowns like he was hosting his own episode of *MTV Cribs*. But the fans? Man, they were worse than the Macarena.

You couldn't escape them. Not at school, not at the mall, not even logged into the old school America Online message boards (CowboysFan69, we know who you are).

It's funny that after all these years the things that come to mind aren't the greatness of one of the NFL's truly great teams. Not the sight of Troy dropping back to either hand to his HOF running back or throw to his HOF receiver or buy time behind his HOF offensive line... no... it was of the obnoxious Cowboys fan at lunch with his barely broken in Game hat telling you how proud he was of *his* team for beating the Falcons or whoever.

If you were a fan, congrats on your wins (and I admit, it's been pretty rough since), but if you weren't? Well, you had to grit your teeth through the loudest, proudest, most short-term loyal fans football has ever seen.

#49

The Program

If you played high school or college football in the early 90s, *The Program* was too good to be true.

A movie about a wild ass FSU-style college football team? In.

That wild-ass FSU football team had James Caan as the coach? And iconic quotes and hits and characters that you emulated in your own locker room? All. The. Way. In.

Rather than telling you (reminding you) about how incredible this movie was for this column, I'm going to run through my seven favorite scenes and quotes that are still as iconic as your old favorite Game hat.

Film Room with Alvin Mack

"2nd and 2 on our own 24, what defensive set?"

"Eagle Zipper Hero, unless the setback shifts into the I."

"Good. 3rd & 7?"

"Oakie Thunder Lion."

"What's your assignment?"

"Kill the quarterback. Hit the tight end so hard his girlfriend dies. Kill everybody."

Alvin Freaking Mack, ladies and gentleman. Flat out legend.

Darnell Jefferson's Cocky Entrance

"Darnell Jefferson, tailback."

"Ray Griffen, starting tailback."

"I know, that's why they recruited me."

Nothing like stepping into the locker room with swagger that could rival Deion Sanders in his prime and going after the starting running back's job AND girlfriend. Darnell ruled.

Joe Kane's Huddle Rally

"Let's put the women and children to bed and go lookin' for fuckin' dinner."

According to my research, this line was repeated in roughly 55,639 high school football huddles in 1993.

Alvin Mack, Fired Up

"Let's open up a can of kick ass and kill them all... Let the paramedics sort 'em out."

Another banger from Alvin Mack, the unofficial greatest college football player of the 90s.

Coach Winters' Injury Inquiry

"Are you injured or are you hurt?"

"What's that mean?"

"If you're hurt, you can still play. If you're injured, you can't."

This exchange was (and is) a gift to every single football coach who ever lived. It's repeated endlessly. It makes total sense. It works. It's genius. I even use it as a dad. Kid falls and won't get up: "Are you injured or are you hurt?"

Lattimer's Insane Celebration

"Starting defense! Seat at the table!"

Right after smashing his head through a car window, Lattimer declared his spot on the starting defense. This is maybe the most insane scene in the film (aside from the one that got cut with the kids laying down on the highway between cars).... However, by this point we knew Lattimer, and somehow breaking a car window with his forehead made sense.

The Spit

Alvin Mack and Steve Lattimer. Spitting in each other's mouths to prove... what exactly? Brotherhood? Toughness? Grossness?

This is one of the iconic scenes from this movie that NEVER was repeated. Thankfully. (And if you did repeat it for some absurd reason, I'm sure you've never told a soul haha).

If you were one of the lucky ones who piled into the theater opening night, or if you've ever put the women and children to bed before going out to get your win, then you know exactly what *The Program* meant to 90s teen dudes back in the day.

#48

Mortal Kombat

W e can't talk about *Street Fighter* (next column) without immediately putting it side-by-side with *Mortal Kombat*. These two games were like the Coke and Pepsi of the 90s arcade world—fierce rivals that defined the era's video game culture. Sure, you probably had a favorite—maybe you were more of a *Street Fighter* purist, or maybe you preferred the darker, bloodier edge of *Mortal Kombat*. Either way, both games carved out their own legendary spaces.

While *Street Fighter* gave us clean, skill-based combat, *Mortal Kombat* cranked everything up to eleven, dripping with violence, blood, and R-rated gore that made it the edgier, "grown-up" game. It wasn't just about beating your opponent—it was about obliterating them. I mean, who could forget Sub-Zero freezing his opponent solid and then shattering them to pieces, or Scorpion decapitating someone or scorching their body with fire like it was just another Tuesday afternoon?

Here's the thing: Street Fighter was like the PG-13 action movie—intense, fun, but still kinda clean. *Mortal Kombat* was the gritty, R-rated horror movie you snuck into when your parents weren't paying attention. The fights were about slaughter; about humiliating your friends with that final knockout blow, teed up by the famous two words: *Finish Him*.

Also, *Mortal Kombat* was built for shit-talking. There was no better feeling than pulling off a perfectly timed Fatality, standing up from the couch or arcade machine, flexing in front of your friend, and knowing you just straight-up killed them. Whether you were tearing out spines or burning your opponent to a crisp with Liu Kang's fireballs, the game was pure adrenaline.

Sonya Blade. Kano. Jax. Kitana. Johnny Cage. Kung Lao. Raiden. Reptile. Sub-Zero.

Mortal Kombat had a deep roster of kick-ass characters, which is why 90s dorm rooms, living rooms, and arcades were filled with the sounds of button-mashing, trash talking, and fatalities galore. It was a pixelated bloodbath and we loved it.

#47

Street Fighter

P icture yourself in seventh grade, rolling into the local arcade with a pocket full of quarters and Zack Morris-level cockiness. You walk through the aisles, the flashing lights from *Pac-Man* and *Galaga* lighting the way like some kind of first generation video game runway, with kids hunched over machines as if they were landing planes.

Then, there it is, in the back of the arcade: the holy grail of early 90s gaming—*Street Fighter II*. A wide-screen stand with two joysticks, buttons begging to be mashed, and that blazing title across the top. This was it. Winner stays on. Simple as that. Lose? You're back to the bench, watching some other kid dominate with your favorite character.

And we *all* had our favorite character. Maybe you were a Chun-Li player like me—spinning bird kick, high knee to the face, lightning fast. Or maybe you were one of those *"Hadouken"* guys, rocking Ken or Ryu, firing off energy balls like a champ.

You could've been a *Sonic Boom* specialist with Guile, flattening your opponents with that perfect haircut and U.S. Army style. Maybe you liked the wild unpredictability of Blanka, electrocuting your way through fights, or Dhalsim's absurd reach that felt unfair but punishing at the same time.

No matter who you picked, you believed you were unbeatable. Whether it was head-to-head with your buddies at home or taking on the nearly impossible M. Bison in challenge mode, *Street Fighter* prowess was a badge of honor. The arcade was where you proved your worth—whether you wiped the floor with your friends or got wrecked by that one kid who seemingly never left the arcade. You know the one, standing there like a boss, with an endless line of challengers feeding his ego and quarters.

But here's the thing: you still have those skills. You might be older now, the arcades may have faded away, but deep down, those joystick moves? They're still in your muscle memory. It's time to get back in the game and remind yourself—and maybe your kids—that you were once a *Street Fighter* legend.

#46

Brett Favre

It's tough to reconcile now, given Brett Favre's post-retirement nosedive into welfare scandals, bad decisions, and increasingly questionable character. But if you lived through the 90s, you know exactly what I mean when I say there was a time when Brett Favre was the go-to "favorite player not on your team" guy in the NFL.

And if you were to ask John Madden, the voice of football back then, who his favorite player to call games for was, the answer was always Brett Favre. Madden would hit you with that line we all knew was coming: "He's just a big kid out there." And he was.

Favre played football like it was recess and no one told him to come back inside. You never knew what was going to happen when he dropped back to pass. He'd scramble, spin, launch a 70-yard rocket off one foot, and you'd either be left cheering or covering your eyes. He could throw six touchdowns or six interceptions in a game, and somehow, you still expected him to pull out a win. That's how un-predictable and flat-out *fun* he was to watch. Every play felt like the final seconds of a backyard game where everyone goes deep, and Favre was the kid drawing it up in the dirt.

He was a three-time MVP, and beyond the field, he was everywhere: commercials, interviews, and, of course, his cameo in *There's Some-thing About Mary*. The Farrelly Brothers could've picked any football star for that role, but they chose Brett Favre, because in the 90s, Brett was *that guy*.

When the Green Bay Packers were constantly contending, Favre sat on top of the NFL pyramid, and every kid watching him dreamed of playing football like that.

Now, seeing the fall from grace is sad. But for those of us who lived through the 90s, Brett Favre will always be a singular part of that era's NFL joy.

Say it ain't so, Brett Fav-rah.

#45

The NWO

If you grew up in the golden era of WWF wrestling in the 1980s, you had your heroes: Hulk Hogan, Macho Man Randy Savage, Ricky "The Dragon" Steamboat, Hacksaw Jim Duggan, Andre the Giant, Rowdy Roddy Piper, Junkyard Dog—the legends of sports entertainment.

For a lot of us 90s kids, these guys were larger-than-life icons. But as the middle of the decade rolled around, something changed. We hit middle school and high school, started getting into our own sports, and got distracted by something called *girls*.

Wrestling took a backseat as we became more passionate about mainstream sports like football, basketball, and baseball. Many of us drifted away from the ring, leaving our childhood wrestling obsessions behind.

And then, something incredible happened.

If you tuned back into the WWE during the late 90s, you were suddenly hit with an attitude adjustment. The Attitude Era was in full swing, and it was glorious. This wasn't the family-friendly, cartoonish wrestling of our youth. No, this was the era of Stone Cold Steve Austin, The Rock, D-Generation X, and Triple H. It was raw (literally and figuratively). It was edgy. It was like watching your childhood favorite comic book characters grow up and start flipping the bird. They even had wet t-shirt contests in the middle of the ring!

But even crazier? If you flipped the channel over to WCW's *Monday Nitro*, you were hit with a jolt of nostalgia like no other. Your childhood heroes—the same Hulk Hogan and Macho Man Randy Savage you grew up worshiping—were *still i*n the ring. But they weren't the squeaky-clean, neon-wearing good guys you remembered. The Macho Man wasn't the hot-pink and purple pants-peddling babyface anymore. Hulk Hogan sported a black and blonde beard, turned heel and was now a member of the NWO (New World Order) with Kevin Nash and Scott Hall. Suddenly, wrestling was back in your life in the most badass way possible. We had offshoots like the Wolfpac. We had Sting. We had Goldberg. We had it all.

Between the propaganda, the vignettes, the threats and the unforgettable feuds and black and white logo, you couldn't take your eyes off the screen.

The Monday Night Wars between WWE and WCW were like nothing else. Raw, Nitro, and eventually *SmackDown!* were must-see TV, full of shit-talking, chaos, and a countercultural vibe that pulled you right back into the wrestling world you thought you'd left behind. It was like an ongoing reality show with your childhood idols in the middle of it.

Sure, WCW is long gone now, but the memories of flipping back and forth between channels, trying to keep up with the madness? Those will last forever.

#44

White Men Can't Jump

We begin with a simple fact: most white men cannot jump as high as they'd like. That's not a stereotype, it's just physics. The title of *White Men Can't Jump* is a statement unto itself, and one that had every white 90s kid who dreamed of throwing down Dominique-level windmills nodding in agreement.

Sure, there are exceptions—Brent Barry winning the dunk contest back in the day, and more recently, Mac McClung making white hoopers proud with his hops—but for the majority of the basketball-playing Caucasian community, a vertical leap over 24 inches is about as likely as becoming an NBA All-Star.

And that's what made *White Men Can't Jump* such a brilliant, one-of-a-kind movie. It centered around two streetball players—Woody Harrelson's Billy Hoyle, a streetwise Larry Bird-type, with slick passes and deadeye shooting, and Wesley Snipes' Sidney Deane, a smooth-talking, trash-talking guard who looked like he walked off an And1 Mixtape, years before those were even a thing.

Here's the kicker: in 1992, Hollywood wasn't making too many sports movies. We'd be lucky to get 3-4 a year, with most of them in the Mighty Ducks, Disney-fied version of storytelling.

So the very fact that a basketball movie about a white guy and a black guy teaming up for pick-up hoops and two-on-two tournaments exists is a win. And the fact that it was good is almost hard to believe even to this day.

White Men Can't Jump hit on every note of 90s basketball culture, from the mythology of streetball legends to the trash-talking, fast-paced action on the court.

Woody Harrelson, fresh off *Cheers*, and Wesley Snipes, fresh off *New Jack City*, were the perfect duo. The first time they meet, they size each other up in a shooting contest, and Woody drops the perfect trash talk line, "I've hustled better players than you, Sidney." It's one of those lines that still brings a smile to our faces.

And then there's the Rosie Perez factor—Woody's fiery, Jeopardy-loving girlfriend who feels like she could do 10x better than Woody, but sticks with him (most of the time). Their chemistry made the off-court scenes just as memorable as the hoop sequences.

But the real magic?

Wesley and Woody, Sydney and Billy, learning to play together and respect each other. This movie captured the energy, the hustle, and the magic of playground hoops. Nothing like it has been made since—and likely, nothing ever will.

#43

Domino's Delivery

I know what you're thinking:

"Domino's delivery, Finkel? Really?"

But if that's where your brain stopped, you're not thinking hard enough. Yes, Domino's delivery!

For a young dude in the 90s—whether you were in middle school, early high school, or anywhere in between—there was no bigger guarantee of an amazing night than getting the parents out of the house, having some friends over, and noticing a crisp 20-dollar bill left on the counter for you to order a large pizza and a liter of Coke.

Domino's wasn't just pizza—it was *freedom*.

Domino's delivery saved you from the endless cycle of peanut butter and jelly sandwiches, the dreaded grilled cheese, or worse, the half-empty bag of Doritos and box of Wheat Thins that were supposed to somehow sustain you for the night. It was a revelation—a way to bring hot, cheesy goodness right to your front door without stepping foot outside.

And back in the 90s, there wasn't Uber Eats or DoorDash. You couldn't just get anything delivered to your house. When you were home alone at 13, 14, 15 or 16, and the only thing you wanted was pizza, unless you had an older sibling or friend's parent willing to drive you to the local pizzeria, you were stuck. That's where Domino's came in like a superhero with a cape made of pepperoni.

Picking up the phone, dialing Domino's, and ordering *exactly* what you wanted—extra cheese, sausage, maybe even some breadsticks or cookies if you were feeling frisky—was a rite of passage. You ordered it, they delivered it, and you paid the delivery guy like a grown-up.

Tossing him a tip?

That was the moment you felt truly in charge.

In a pre-smartphone, pre-delivery-app world, Domino's was teen empowerment. It was autonomy. You couldn't drive yet, but with Domino's, you didn't need to. They brought the good stuff to you. We didn't realize it at the time, but every delivery was a small taste of responsibility.

So here's to you, Domino's. You saved many a night back in the day, and for that, we salute you.

#42

Good Will Hunting

"How do you like them apples?"

If you were a 90s kid, this line probably lives rent-free in your brain, along with the image of Matt Damon's smirk as he one-ups that snobby ponytail dude in *Good Will Hunting*. (And while we're here, don't let me catch any of you reading this regurgitating Gordon Wood. Not on my watch.)

Also, let's not forget the absolutely terrible Boston accents it spawned in dorm rooms and basements across America.

"Chuck I had a double burgah!" might be the most butchered Boston phrase of all time, and we've got Damon and Affleck to thank for that.

But here's the thing: *Good Will Hunting* hit home for us 90s dudes. Yes, it was a movie about a genius with a troubled past—but it was really a window into a group of guys who, in many ways, reminded us of ourselves. Will, Chucky, Billy, Morgan—these guys could've been our older brothers, the dudes just out of high school, grinding it out in blue-collar jobs. They were raw, they busted each other's balls nonstop, and yet they were fiercely loyal. Even if you grew up in the safe confines of the suburbs, you felt connected to them.

Will's genius? Sure, it was impressive, but it wasn't what made us like him. It was the way he used that genius to punk elitists, outwit pompous professors, destroy Ivy League dickheads at their own game and (while this has nothing to do with intelligence), it was fun watching him beat the piss out of Carmine Scarpaglia.

Then you had the emotional backbone of the movie—Robin Williams as the tough-love therapist, giving us the "It's not your fault" moment that still makes the room get a little dusty. There were rumors and conspiracy theories about how the script came to be, with William Goldman's involvement and an edited CIA plot line, but at the end of the day, *Good Will Hunting* was about a group of dudes figuring out life. They worked manual labor jobs, drank beers, chased girls, and above all, stuck together in good times and bad.

Forget being a genius from Southie - that sounded like a great life for a twenty-three year old C+ student from anywhere.

#41

Chris Rock

C hris Rock's 90s rise to superstardom begins with a journey to *Saturday Night Live* following the typical young comedian hustle of the time: grinding the stand-up circuit, getting nods from the right people, and convincing Lorne Michaels to give him a shot at the age of 25.

Suddenly, there he was, on *SNL*, the self-described new "funny Black guy," following in the footsteps of his idol, Eddie Murphy. He quickly fell in with the 90s crew—Sandler, Spade, Farley, Schneider – and most of them have since reunited for what feels like a dozen *Grown Ups* movies.

But unlike Rock's buddies who had signature bits (Sandler's mega-hit songs or Farley's Matt Foley or Schneider's "making copies" or Spade's monologues), Rock never quite landed *that* character or moment. They gave it a shot with stuff like "I'm Chillin'," but nothing felt like it crossed over into the "he'll be known for that zone". And honestly, that's fine because Rock was saving some of his best performances for outside of 30 Rock.

He was great as Pookie in *New Jack City* and he turned a doll into a star with his award-winning Lil' Penny Nike commercials.

But the true magic? Rock on stage with a mic in his hand.

For those of us who were a little too young for Eddie Murphy's *Delirious* or who snuck in some Andrew Dice Clay when our parents weren't around, Chris Rock became *our* guy in 1996 with *Bring the Pain.*

Rock was raw, hilarious, and brilliant. He had that edge and that voice and that sharp social commentary we probably didn't quite understand yet. And of course, hechanged how we hear the phrase "tossing salad" forever. Even to this day, in a restaurant, if a waiter mentions tossed salad my mind goes back to this bit. Gross.

After *Bring the Pain*, he closed out the 90s with another standup special, *Bigger & Blacker,* which taught all of us important health lessons, like how even severe injuries can be healed by rubbin' some 'tussin on them.

But in between those two signature shows, Rock gave what I still believe to be his best performance in a movie, playing Lee Butters in *Lethal Weapon IV*. He was the perfect foil for Danny Glover's Murtaugh, brought the laughs with Mel Gibson's Riggs and even held his own in some action scenes.

SNL.

Films.

Stand-up.

Rock was a true 90s triple threat and he deserves our respect.

#40

Jordan IV & Jordan V

A h, the Jordan IV and V sneakers—peak 90s footwear. Nothing said, "I probably can't hoop, but I have rich parents," quite like showing up to middle school gym class or high school pick-up wearing a pair of these.

And even thirty years later the reason I'm still ripping on the kids who had them is because I wanted them so badly, but instead of spending my lawn mowing money on shoes, I saved forever and bought a 5-disc CD changer.

But back to the early 90s Jordans.

Among cool kids with means, the Jordan IV was like the sneaker equivalent of the yellow Sony Sport Walkman: they were everywhere. I remember staring at the screen pattern on the side and above the toes on some other kid's shoes in science class to this day. Those mesh side panels were basically air conditioning for your feet.

Then came the Jordan V in 1990.

Everyone has their own version of Jordan's they think of when the shoes come up in conversation, but I'd guess for most 90s kids, this is the first pair that comes to mind. Partly because they were the coolest looking pair to date - and partly because Spike Lee's character Mars Blackmon introduced them in the commercials that aired non-stop.

Famous Nike designer Tinker Hatfield compared the shoes to WWII fighter planes. Combine that with the shark tooth shaped designs on the midsoles and we have ourselves a shoe equally at home on the basketball court or facing off against Titan in *American Gladiators*. These were also the kicks featured on the infamous *Sports Illustrated* cover for the story about kids being robbed for their shoes called *"Your Sneakers Or Your Life."*

The IVs and Vs were equal parts shoes and status symbols. And while I was never able to do it, if you somehow convinced your parents to spring for a pair back in the day, my hat's off to you. I hope you still have them.

#39

Demolition Man

"*What's your boggle?*"

This has to be one of the goofiest questions ever to be spoken on screen, and yet, it's perfect.

You understand it without understanding why anyone would talk that way. It's English but seems like a version you haven't heard before. It's both foreign and familiar.

And it's also the ultimate litmus test for dudes to see if another dude is their kind of dude.

For instance:

You could be walking your dog, sitting on the sidelines at your kid's soccer game, or just bumping into some random guy on the street and as awkward as it might sound, if you decide to drop a, "What's your boggle?", you're going to instantly know if he's seen *Demolition Man* or not.

If he hasn't, he'll ask, "Um, what?"

If he has, he'll say, "Haha did you just reference *Demolition Man*? I love that movie."

Needless to say, the second exchange is how you know you've found a 90s action aficionado kindred spirit.

As for the movie itself, *Demolition Man* is unique, peak 90s cinema, featuring two stars at the top of their game: Sylvester Stallone as John Spartan and Wesley Snipes as Simon Phoenix.

First, let's just take a moment to appreciate those names—John Spartan and Simon Phoenix. These aren't just action hero names, they're *Hall of Fame* action hero names.

John Spartan joins the elite ranks of other legendary Johns like John Matrix (*Commando*) and John McClane (*Die Hard*). And Simon Phoenix? That's pure action movie magic—complete with Snipes rocking platinum blonde hair, sleeveless shirts, and crazy eyes.

The premise of *Demolition Man* is also brilliant: it's a future where all the fun of the 90s—fast food, swearing, anything remotely exciting—has been outlawed by a sanitized, overly polite ruling class. Enter John Spartan, the caveman from the past, brought in to stop the maniacal Simon Phoenix from wreaking havoc in this squeaky-clean society.

The action is next level, the fight scenes are epic, and you've got Dennis Leary leading an underground rebellion of rat burger-eating rebels (Edgar Friendly, another stellar name).

Plus, a young Sandra Bullock as the love interest, and Benjamin Bratt as the hapless cop who has no clue what he's up against. And don't even get me started on the three seashells.

So yes, *Demolition Man* is quintessential 90s—brimming with action, creativity, and the perfect mix of ridiculousness.

Oh, and the next time someone asks, "What's your boggle?"— the perfect response is:

"Mellow greetings."

#38

Mama Said Knock You Out

T his column is a little different from some of the others because not only do I believe that *Mama Said Knock You Out* is the best workout song of the 90s; I think it's the greatest workout song of ALL TIME.

Here is my case:

THE OPEN

Don't call it a comeback!!!

Oh, man. Has there ever been a more definitive, powerful declaration to start a song? Ever? Have the first five words of a song ever been sung with more anger/purpose/built-up rage? Have the first five words of a song ever said so much in so few syllables?

"Don't call it a comeback!" is concise and cutting and is the tip of the spear to the rest of *Mama Said Knock You Out,* LL's verbal nuclear missile aimed at anyone who thought he fell off after his previous album, *Walking with a Panther.*

THE POWDER KEG OF CLASSIC LINES

Don't you dare stare, you betta move,
Don't ever compare,
Me to the rest that'll all get sliced and diced,
Competition's payin' the price...

Who doesn't want to slice and dice the competition? Who doesn't want to make people they're up against pay the price? It's almost as if these words were written with gym rats in mind, giving them an anthem to take out their daily frustrations with punishing deadlifts and slam ball super sets.

Just like Muhummad Ali they called him Cassius
Watch me bash this beat like a skull

Let's give LL some extra credit here for rhyming 'Cassius' with 'bash this' to squeeze an Ali reference into a song about beating up the competition. It's such a clutch move by LL.

Side note: when this song came out I had zero idea who he was referencing because there was no Google and I was 11 and didn't know the history of Ali changing his name. I think I finally understood the 'Cassius' reference early in high school.

I'm blastin, outlastin
Kinda like Shaft, so u could say I'm shaftin'

LL isn't typically discussed in the upper echelon of wordsmiths/MCs, but I'll tip my cap here not only for his ability to work in a Shaft shout out, but for also writing a verse that has Shaft basically rhyming with itself in the same line without it sounding poorly... And I've always liked the "blastin'" and "outlastin'" tag team word combination.

> *I'm goin' insane, startin' the hurricane, releasin' pain'*
> *Lettin 'you know that you can't gain, I maintain*
> *Unless ya say my name*
> *Rippin, killin*
> *Diggin and drillin a hole*
> *Pass the Ol' Gold*

This is my favorite coupling of lyrics in the song. It's the crescendo of LL's anger. He has flat out had enough of people doubting him and he's letting us all know. Workout-wise, the insane-hurricane-pain line can push you through just about any tough lift you're going through if you can time it right. And if you aren't shadow boxing you should be.

> *Don't u neva, eva, pull my lever*
> *Cuz I explode*
> *And my nine is easy to load*
> *I gotta thank God*
> *Cuz he gave me the strength to rock*
> *HARD!!*

Perfect ending to the perfect pump-up song. It's got three or four stop-and-starts that explode like grenades: *Neva! Eva! Pull my lever!* But it somehow keeps building momentum to a powerful finish... And who doesn't want the strength to rock... Hard!!!

THE VIDEO

LL Cool J. Alone in a boxing ring. Wearing a hoodie. Spitting (and literally spitting) all over a mic.

The intensity on his half-covered face is genuine. The feeling of strength in the ring is palpable. Every word feels like it's being yelled directly at you.

And on top of that you intercut LL singing with shots of him lifting weights and flexing and you've got the gold standard in terms of a motivational workout video and song. And this wasn't even the super-jacked, super-fit version of LL we have today. This was the in-great-shape, about-to-be-swole, version of LL.

THE TITLE

I know the rumor about how this song got started is that LL's grandmother told him to go knock out his competition. I think it's even been verified in places. If it's true, great. If not, no big deal. It's a phenomenal title either way.

Essentially, every meathead wants to knock someone out and if you have your grandmother's permission, all the better.

THE CHORUS & BEAT

Excellent and more excellent. I love the repetition of 'Mama Said Knock You Out' and 'I'm Gonna Knock You Out'... It's like LL just keeps confirming that he got the request, heard it and is gonna act... Hard!!!

And the beat... It's steady. It's strong. It never lets up. Love all of it. There's honestly nothing about the song I don't enjoy and it's impossible to not bob your head a bit the second the first beat drops.

Personally, I've taken LL's advice. I do not call this a regular jam. I call this the best workout jam ever.

#37

Citrus Cooler Gatorade

C itrus Cooler Gatorade is, without a doubt, the greatest flavor of any flavored thing of all time. Better than banana Laffy Taffy. Better than watermelon Jolly Ranchers. Better than them all.

If you grew up in the '90s, you already know this. It's not just about the taste—it's about the feeling you got every time you cracked open one of those neon orange bottles. And not just the lame plastic bottles you get today. I'm talking about the heavy, grooved glass bottles that Gatorade was meant to be drunk from.

Citrus Cooler was the ultimate drink for driveway hoops, long afternoons of wiffle, NBA Jam dominated late-night sleepovers, and after-school hangouts when MTV mattered and you envied the kid in your neighborhood who had Reebok pumps.

What made Citrus Cooler so glorious wasn't just its unique mix of that unnameable citrus flavor —it was that it fit seamlessly into the rhythm of growing up in the '90s.

We weren't glued to our phones, obsessing over Instagram stories; we were out there actually living life, and Citrus Cooler was our drink of choice. This was the flavor that fueled us while we convinced our friends to trade us a Mark McGwire Team USA baseball card for a Bo Jackson Rated Rookie.

And don't forget, you couldn't just find it everywhere either, which somehow made it even better. It was like a secret code for true Gatorade fans—if you showed up to practice with a Citrus Cooler, you were immediately on another level. It wasn't about flashy new flavors, or weird limited-edition gimmicks. It was consistent, reliable, and absolutely delicious.

And let's be real: it tasted like winning because we all knew it was Michael Jordan's favorite flavor. Whether you were dominating a pick-up game or just surviving the chaos of gym class, Citrus Cooler made it all feel like a victory. Every sip brought you back to those golden afternoons when the biggest worry was whether you could stay up late enough to catch the SportsCenter Top 10.

Gatorade has tried a million flavors since: ice, frosted, zero and on and on. But Citrus Cooler will always be #1. And even more important, it blows away whatever super sweet nonsense Logan Paul is pouring into those neon Prime bottles.

#36

Barry Sanders

There was a debate in the 90s that seemed to pop up at every lunch table, every backyard football game, and every conversation with your buddies who thought they were NFL experts: Who was the better running back—Emmitt Smith or Barry Sanders? Now, don't get me wrong, Emmitt was a beast. But the logic always went something like this: Emmitt had everything—an entire offensive line made of Pro Bowlers, a Pro Bowl tight end, a Pro Bowl fullback, a Pro Bowl quarterback. Hell, the Cowboys were an All-Star team in the early 90s – *of course,* Emmitt racked up yards.

It would've been a bigger surprise if he didn't.

But Barry?

Barry Sanders was on an island. He was the Detroit Lions' entire offense for years. And despite playing on a team that was kind of a disaster most seasons, he still cranked out 1,000-yard and 1,500-yard seasons like clockwork. Barry Sanders was the most electric football player of the early 90s. Those of us who missed the Walter Payton years, or only caught flashes of Bo Jackson before he got hurt, knew one thing: Barry was on a different level.

You can close your eyes right now and picture it: Number 20 in that blue Lions jersey, spinning, juking, stopping on a dime—then stopping again—losing seven yards just to sprint 40 up the sideline for a touchdown. At times, it seemed like his feet weren't even touching the ground. He was playing turbo mode while everyone else was stuck playing under water. When you hit the playground with your friends, every kid had their own "Barry Sanders" spin move in their head, even if none of us had any idea what we were doing.

In the 90s, the Cowboys, 49ers, and Broncos might've dominated the Super Bowls, but Barry? Barry dominated our imaginations. And let's not forget, there was no NFL RedZone or streaming service. You couldn't just catch a Lions game whenever you wanted. You had to wait for SportsCenter—wait for Chris Berman's "Top 10 Plays" every Sunday—to get your Barry fix. And dammit, it was always worth the wait.

#35

GoldenEye 007

Two questions:

How many video games have famous pause music?

How many video games have famous pause music that you remember 30 freaking years later?

Don't bother trying to answer. I'm sure some of you can come up with one or two, depending on how much time you spent on your Nintendo64 or XBox or PlayStation...

BUT...

The correct answer here is one: *GoldenEye 007*

The bass. The echoes. The house beats.

Hitting pause in this game made you feel like you'd just entered a secret club in New York City that you didn't belong in.

Then the xylophone taps hit and took this entire soundtrack to the next level.

I knew dudes in college who just left this damn pause music on repeat in their dorms and fraternity rooms while they hung out because it rocked so hard.

And we haven't even gotten to the game yet!

First person shooter.

Sniper rifles. Grenades. Throwing knives. Pistols. The Klobb submachine guns. You legit felt like Bond out there.

And not only did you need to reload the weapons like in real life, but your aim and precision and skills mattered.'

Head shots were killers.

Leg shots kept your enemy alive.

You've gotta maneuver through nuclear silos, Russian winters, mansions, castles, jungles and more, all while avoiding the henchman of General Arkady Ourumov.

There were levels it took you days to beat.

Sequences you couldn't quite master.

Missions you fell short on.

You'd get to the final stage at the control center for the GoldenEye radio telescope and die.

But you kept trying and fighting until the job was done, just like the real James Bond... Because when you were immersed in this game, you were 007.

#34

Taco Bell Bacon Cheeseburger Burrito

In the wild west of 90s fast food, where every franchise was throwing caution (and ingredients) to the wind, there was one mad scientist who truly reigned supreme: Taco Bell.

This was an era when fast food joints were on an absolute power trip, experimenting with their menus like they were auditioning for a spot on *Bill Nye the Science Guy*. McDonald's had its infamous McLean Deluxe, Burger King tried a gross, elongated Italian sausage sandwich, and the ill-fated Big King and Fiesta Whopper. Wendy's gave us a country fried steak sandwich and the Carolina Classic with coleslaw (tasted like you'd expect).

But no one—*no one*—went as hard as Taco Bell. After trying to combat their burger rivals with a sloppy joe-styled sandwich called the "Bell Beefer", which was essentially two burger buns filled with Taco Bell meat, they realized that in order to win, they didn't need to compete with McDonald's at their game, they needed to take the burger game and make it their own.

And thus, they took the very essence of fast food rebellion and said, "Why make burgers when we can turn burgers into burritos?"

Genius!

That's how the Taco Bell double bacon cheeseburger burrito was born. This was the true masterpiece; the pièce de résistance.

Forget about the nutritional value of this culinary Frankenstein monster (spoiler: there wasn't any). We're here to talk about this bacon cheeseburger burrito being the anchor to an all-star Taco Bell offering.

Kids today have no idea what it was like to be a starving, ravenous 14-year-old in the mid-90s, rolling up to Taco Bell with a crisp $10 bill burning a hole in your pocket.

This was the golden era of fast food economics—where you could walk into a T-Bell and practically *dare* yourself to spend all $10. For less than an Alexander Hamilton, you could roll out of a drive thru with three gorditas, a couple of massive tacos, a Mexican pizza and maybe two bacon cheeseburger burritos, all for about the same price as a CD single.

Inflation has since ruined this glorious scenario, but back then? It was an all-you-can-eat dream we all wish we could go back to.

#33

Terminator 2

When you talk about the bands that dominated the 90s, there's no way to leave out Guns N' Roses. Sure, grunge came in and took over the airwaves with Nirvana and Pearl Jam, but before that, GNR exploded onto the scene with *Appetite for Destruction*, an album that was more than music - it was a force of nature.

You had Paradise City, Nighttrain, Welcome to the Jungle, Mr. Brownstone and more, all one one album that screamed edge, anger, and straight-up hard ass music.

So when Arnold Schwarzenegger, the biggest action star of the early 90s, teamed up with James Cameron, the biggest action director of the era, to make *Terminator 2*, who else would they turn to for the signature song on the soundtrack but Guns N' Roses?

It was a match made in every dude's cinematic and musical dream.

You've got a jacked Arnold in a leather jacket and sunglasses, riding a Harley, flip-cocking a shotgun, and blasting away at the futuristic, shape-shifting T-1000 made of liquid metal alloy. Oh, and he's doing all of this while saving humanity from the looming threat of Skynet.

T-2 is the perfect combination of mind-blowing action, next-level special effects, and a surprisingly deep theme of machine vs. man, with AI learning what it means to care, to have heart, and to understand why humans cry.

But what ties it all together, making it quintessentially 90s, is that iconic scene where Arnold rolls in, and the backdrop is blaring with Guns N' Roses' *You Could Be Mine*.

Explosions, motorcycles, shotguns, *plus* GNR? It's like someone bottled pure 90s adrenaline and injected it into a film, then into your veins.

If you were 13, 15, or 17 when you saw *Terminator 2* in theaters, you probably remember that experience to this day. Hasta la vista, baby.

#32

MTV's
Rock 'N Jock

I f there was ever a perfect fusion of pop culture, sports, and pure 90s coolness, it was MTV's *Rock N' Jock*. Long before social media gave us constant glimpses into the private lives of athletes and celebrities, *Rock N' Jock* was the ultimate window into a world we couldn't see.

Back then, there was no Instagram feed of your favorite basketball player chilling with your favorite actor, or videos of musicians throwing a football around with athletes on the sideline.

As 90s kids, we had no access to those behind-the-scenes moments, no #SquadGoals. And then, out of nowhere, *Rock N' Jock* stepped in and blew our minds.

The first MTV softball game featuring the Aardvarks versus the Salamanders included an impossible mix of A-listers across genres.

The Aardvarks' infield showcased Poison's Bret Michaels, the Reds' Barry Larkin and actor Corbin Bernsen. The outfield had Mark McGwire, MC Hammer, singer Belinda Carlisle and Keanu Reeves.

The Salamanders likewise had a powerful celeb squad, with Tone Loc, Kevin Costner and Wally Joyner in the infield and Daryl Strawberry in the outfield.

And the teams only got better from there.

By the time the team names changed to the Home Boys and the Away Boys, the biggest names in entertainment were begging to play. The 1994 softball game alone featured Chuck D, Ken Griffey Jr., Jon Bon Jovi, Dwight Gooden, Treach and Gary Scheffield in one dugout with Dan Cortese, Frank Thomas, Barry Bonds, and all three ladies from Salt-N-Pepa in the other.

Where else could you see someone like Jon Bon Jovi hit a pop fly to Griffey who then threw to Bret Michaels at first to get Heather Locklear in a rundown?

"Nowhere", is the answer.

Yes, they kept score.

But these games weren't about the score.

They were about seeing worlds collide. Supermodels, rock stars, athletes—all hanging out like it was no big deal.

For us, though? It was a HUGE deal, both for the obvious star power reasons and, as dudes, we also loved figuring out if our favorite musicians and actors were any good at sports.

Could they actually play, or were they just trying not to embarrass themselves?

This was more fun with the Rock 'N Jock basketball series, which took the stakes to another level because if you played ball you could *instantly* tell whether one of these celebs had skills.

What did their shot look like? How did they dribble? Were they comfortable passing and playing D?

You could fake it on the softball field, but hoops?

Nope.

When Queen Latifah is crossing dudes over and Jaleel White (Urkel himself!) is putting on a clinic, you knew it was serious. Suddenly, every kid shooting hoops in their driveway was thinking, "I could totally dominate if I was out there against NBA All-Stars."

The beauty of *Rock N' Jock* was that it made these larger-than-life celebrities feel a little more real. You'd watch, imagine yourself out there, and think, "Yeah, I could definitely take Marky Mark off the dribble."

#31

Regulate

The story of *Regulate* begins like so many great epic tales in literature:

"It was a clear black night, a clear white moon, Warren G was on the streets trying to consume..."

And if you stopped there, you'd think you were about to hear a story about an evening of good times and smooth rides and pretty ladies by a young gentleman with the first name 'Warren' and the last name 'G'.

But this is *Regulate*, and as any 90s kid knows, it's less about Warren G's street prowess and more about Nate Dogg's timely intervention.

Okay. I'm being kind.

Warren G did precious little regulating in this song. In fact, Warren spent most of the night getting punked and being bailed out by Nate Dogg—who, fortunately, was rolling around with 16 in the clip and one in the hole, ready to make some bodies turn cold.

If Warren G had been left to his own devices, he might have ended up with no car, no money, no ladies, and maybe worse. But that's where Nate Dogg comes in—cool, calm, and deadly—saving the day and letting Warren G live to tell the tale.

Originally from the *Above the Rim* soundtrack in 1994, *Regulate* soon became so much bigger than its movie roots. It's one of those songs that sticks with you forever—the smooth cadence of Warren G's verses, Nate Dogg's legendary voice, and that unbeatable beat.

For a time, *Regulate* was everywhere, turning Warren G into an artist in his own right rather than that guy you always saw on Snoop and Dre's videos. To this day it remains his career-defining track, and if you're cruising around in your car listening to a 90s station and that whistle hits... Damn!

There's only three words that pop into your head:

Regulators! Mount Up!

#30

Grant Hill

G rant Hill was squeaky clean—literally and metaphorically. He was the one Duke guy that everyone had to respect, even if you were a Duke hater, which, let's be honest, was and is just about all of us.

Christian Laettner? The guy had a face that made you want to crane kick a hole through your dad's 400-lb big screen TV.

Bobby Hurley? Slapping the floor on defense like he was Donkey Kong? What a dickhead.

But Grant Hill? He was different.

He was polished. Poised. Played the game hard without being obnoxious like most Coach K disciples.

He was the athlete you couldn't help but appreciate. He was dubbed the "Next Jordan" while in college and most people didn't argue too much about it at the time.

Was it a stretch? Probably

Was it out of the realm of possibility? No.

When Grant Hill was selected as the 3rd overall pick in the 1994 NBA Draft (same pick as Jordan) by the Detroit Pistons, the expectations were through the roof. It had been five years since the Bad Boys had left town and now they brought in a good dude to turn things around.

And Hill started to.

In no time, he was a Rookie of the Year, All-Star, First Team All-NBA and he took Detroit from 20 wins his first year to 54 in the '96-'97 season.

Along the way Hill became a marketing giant and instead of signing with sneaker titans like Nike or Reebok, Grant made a baller move. He threw his lot in with...Fila.

Yeah, Fila, the brand that, up until then, was better known for Euro tennis shoes and tracksuits.

But, believe it or not, for a stretch there, it worked. The Grant Hill Fila 1s and 2s? They were legit. They may not have been Jordans, Iverson's Questions, or Shaq's Shaqnosis, but in the mid-90s, they held their own in sneaker culture.

Grant Hill wasn't just being compared to Jordan on the court—he was being marketed like him too. Sprite commercials (who can forget 1-800-Tall-Men with Tim Duncan), sneaker ads, Nestle Crunch bill-boards, magazine covers—he was everywhere. For a few glorious years, Hill was a bona fide superstar, poised to take over the NBA narrative.

Then: Injuries.

A bunch of them.

Sucks.

Who knows what might have been if Hill was able to stay at his peak for 6-10 years? Championships? Maybe? We'll never know.

One thing is for sure, though.

You can't tell the story of the 90s NBA without Grant Hill and his brief, shining moment as basketball's next big thing.

#29

Saved By the Bell

"*When I wake up in the mornin',*
And the 'larm gives out a warnin',
I don't think I'll ever make it on time,
By the time I grab my books,
And I give myself a look,
I'm at the corner just in time to see the bus fly by!
It's alright 'cuz I'm saved by the bell."

First, a confession:

I did a search for the *'Saved By the Bell'* lyrics for this column and not once, ever, in the thousand times I heard this song did I think the words in the second stanza were, *"and the 'larm gives out a warnin'"*

I don't even know what I thought the second line was... I kind of just skipped it and jumped right into the "make it on time... grab my books... give myself a look..." section...

Am I alone in this?

Did you actually know the second line?

Most likely, it didn't matter, because as catchy as the theme song was, nothing on wholesome 90s TV encapsulated the bizarre yet oddly relatable high school experience quite like *Saved by the Bell.*

You had your trio of teen guy archetypes: Zack Morris, AC Slater, and Screech—aka the cool guy (or preppie), the jock, and the dork. Although, most of the time, 90s archetypically speaking, the cool guy *was* the jock... but that's splitting hairs.

The holy trinity of high school stereotypes at Bayside wasn't designed to reflect reality. It was designed to help you escape from reality so that you'd stop and think, "Wait, was my high school supposed to be like this?"

Let's start with the dudes:

Zack was the ultimate 90s high school TV stud—handsome, always scheming, rarely caught, and flashing that giant cell phone as an accessory to his awesomeness.

AC Slater was the muscle-bound, wrestler / football player / jock, constantly flexing his biceps and sporting pants that screamed, "I'm athletic, but I might also have dance class at 3."

Then there was Screech—oh, poor Screech—forever chasing girls way out of his league, trying to prove that geeks on TV could somehow be best friends with the coolest guys in school, even though in reality, they probably sat five lunch tables apart.

And now onto the ladies of Bayside.

Kelly Kapowski was the all-American dream girl who 40% of 90s dudes point to as their first TV crush.

Lisa Turtle was the fashion queen with a side of sass.

And Jessie Spano was the OCD, caffeine-pill-popping overachiever whose "I'm so excited!" meltdown became as iconic as any other 90s moment.

Each character had a lane, and 94% of the time, they stayed in it.

But the real magic of *Saved by the Bell* was the chemistry. These frenemies might've fought over dates or school trophies, but they always came together in the end. It was a sugary sweet, gloriously cheesy look into a high school experience that didn't exist but made you wish it did.

#28

Nic Cage

In the annals of 90s action films, one man surprisingly emerged to dominate the genre in a way that makes you want to shout "Put the bunny back in the box!"—and that isn't Sly Stallone or Wesley Snipes or Arnold.

No.

That man is none other than the great Nicolas Cage, who turned an Oscar win for playing an alcoholic in *Leaving Las Vegas* into three movies that had zero chance at winning Oscars, but a 100% chance that you were going to opening night.

Forget comic book IP, forget toys, forget franchises...

Cage, in the mid-to-late '90s, went on a cinematic heater so hot you could cook a rack of Totino's pizza rolls on it. We're talking about one outrageous blockbuster after another, where Cage somehow managed to blend intensity, absurdity, and straight-up coolness into roles that have become iconic.

It all starts with *The Rock* (1996).

The premise alone is absurd: A group of rogue military operatives takes over Alcatraz, holds tourists hostage, and tries to force the U.S. government to meet their demands or they'll launch chemical-weapons at San Francisco.

Enter Stanley Goodspeed (Cage), an awkward FBI chemical expert, paired with none other than Sean Connery—a genius ex-con who just happens to be the only man ever to escape The Rock. Together, they battle VX gas and a slew of disgruntled ex-marines. It's part buddy-cop flick, part prison break movie, and all Cage awesomeness. This could've been the only film Cage made in the '90s, and he'd still be in the Action Movie Hall of Fame.

But nope, Cage was just getting started.

Next up, *Con Air* (1997), which has an even more ridiculous premise: A prison transport plane full of America's worst criminals goes haywire, and the only man who can stop them is—you guessed it—Cameron Poe, an impossibly jacked, long-haired, slow-talking Cage.

This movie has it all: plane crashes in Vegas, John Malkovich in peak evil mode, John Cusack as a desperate, exasperated good guy, Steve Buscemi as a serial killer you kinda root for, and even a young Dave Chappelle getting crushed to death by the closing hangar on the plane.

And the piece de resistance of Cage's 90's run is *Face/Off* (incredibly, also 1997), the film that pushed action movie premise lunacy to new heights.

Directed by John Woo, *Face/Off* features Cage and John Travolta literally switching faces. That's the whole premise—Cage as a bad guy becomes the good guy, Travolta as a good guy becomes the bad guy, and chaos ensues. It's as ridiculous as it sounds and yet because of both actors going all-in and some incredible John Woo action sequences, the movie is somehow one of the most captivating and memorable action films of all time.

The Rock. Con Air. Face/Off.

Well done, 90s Nic Cage.

Well done.

And thank you for giving us the the perfect lead in to a tough question:

"How in the name of Zeus's butthole...!"

#27

Beavis & Butthead

"*I am the Great Cornholio! I need TP for my bunghole!*"

The fact that you're already laughing proves how much of a stranglehold Beavis and Butthead had on your brain in high school. No duo captured the basic, bare bones, laugh-at-dumb stuff teenage boy humor quite like these two knuckleheads.

Whether it was Beavis with his high-pitched, maniacal giggle, or Butthead with his slow, belly and chest drawling chuckle, you couldn't help but sit on your couch and watch them sit on their couch and laugh as they ripped on music videos, smacked each other and affectionately called each other "buttmunch".

For a generation of dudes over the age of 13, this was must-see television. Beavis and Butthead embodied that glorious mix of low-brow humor, fart jokes, and "dumbass" insults that made us feel like... well... we were watching a version of ourselves.

Their school had an overly intense gym teacher like yours probably did. Whether he yelled, "Kick me in the jimmies!" is besides the point. You had girls who put you down, though you may not have started a "Diarrhea, cha-cha-cha!" chant - unless her name was Daria. And like you, Beavis and Butthead went on random daily adventures into the world of adults that always ended in disaster.

You loved them so much you imitated them.

And you had competitions imitating them.

Maybe you were better at doing Beavis's overly excited "Yeah, yeah!" or Butthead's trademark slow "Heh-heh."

In hindsight, it doesn't matter.

What matters is that right now, as you're reading this, you could probably do that exact imitation spot on.

Even years later, their influence lingers. Recently, *Saturday Night Live* brought them back in a skit with Ryan Gosling and Kenan Thompson, and guess what? It was easily one of the funniest skits they've done in the past 25 years. Beavis and Butthead were, and still are, the kings of dumb, endearing humor.

Two cartoon morons ruling prime-time TV?

What a time to be alive.

#26

Andre Agassi

There was a time, not too long ago, when U.S. men's tennis was undeniably cool, when stars were dominating Wimbledon and the U.S. Open AND pop culture. In the 80s, you had John McEnroe, the tantrum-throwing bad boy with a temper as fast as his serve. But in the 90s? Enter *the* man—Andre Agassi - a bona fide cultural phenomenon.

Agassi didn't show up in tennis whites and wave politely to the crowd. Nah, Andre Agassi showed up in neon pink shirts, electric yellow shorts, and headbands that screamed rockstar rebellion. The guy had a mullet so majestic it could've headlined Lollapalooza. Agassi made tennis, a sport often associated with polite claps and pristine lawns, feel like a U2 concert.

He was the anti-country club player—hailing not from some preppy northern Florida estate, but from Las Vegas, baby. The guy had swagger. He even dated the 80s "It" girl, Brooke Shields, for an early 90s flex.

And when he wasn't gracing center court with another W, he was sharing commercials with the Red Hot Chili Peppers, air-guitaring on his tennis racket like it was a Fender Strat. Oh, and let's not forget those iconic Nike Agassi shoes—hot pink, unapologetically loud. People rocked those things everywhere - even people who you wouldn't expect.

True story: Even my dad, Harvey, once wore a pair of those hot pink Agassis. As an executive. To work! That's how much of a crossover star Andre was. If you had those shoes, you were part of the Agassi rebellion.

Sure, since then, tennis has seen Federer's grace, Nadal's grit, and Djokovic's dominance, but charisma? The kind of electric, in-your-face personality that pulled young dudes away from their Super Nintendo to go grab a tennis racket? That was all Andre.

Why?

Because he lived the famous tagline from his infamous Canon Rebel commercials: Image is Everything.

#25

Madden

There were few things more guaranteed to kick off an epic afternoon in 8th grade than your buddy biking up to your house, knocking on your door and saying the four magic words:

"Dude, wanna play Madden?"

You knew that question meant hours of gaming glory, smack-talking and speed-boosting up the sideline. And it all started with that classic tough guy video game narrator saying:

E! A! Sports! It's in the game.

The cool thing about Madden was that it was a video game AND a crash course in the NFL and football strategy. When picking teams you'd get little updates on how they might do that year, even if they were as lame as the San Diego Chargers' 1995 entry:

"The 1995 Chargers possess a solid defense and a gutsy offense."

You'd also get All-Madden Teams and all-time teams so you could learn a little pigskin history too.

But the real value came in the play calling.

Long before most of us were old enough to put on NFL pads, and definitely long before we were ever going to be calling an offense or defense on the sideline, when you had that controller in your hand, you were your own little Bill Belichick.

On offense you weren't just calling random plays; you were learning about single back formations, I-formations, sweeps, draws, slant-and-gos and more.

On defense you studied up on the 3-4 and the 4-3 and the dime package and nickel package and the all-out blitz and whatever other defensive nuggets were in those six boxes you could choose from.

Madden taught us to think like coaches, GMs, and players, all while giving us the chance to control the greatest players we'd only ever seen on TV.

Sure, some of us cut our teeth on *Tecmo Bowl*, where Bo Jackson was an unstoppable God and Jerry Rice caught literally everything. But Madden? Madden was different. It gave us new heroes.

Randall Cunningham could scramble for what seemed like days, throwing an 80-yard bomb as he sprinted for his life. Barry Sanders spun his way to the end zone, dodging defenders like they were holograms. Steve Young had wheels. John Elway could throw darts and scramble. Michael Irvin never dropped balls.

And then, of course, there were the classic battles: Cowboys vs. 49ers, Falcons with Deion Sanders, or those very late 90s Vikings teams with Randy Moss snatching deep balls all day (I, for one, used to play whole games where I'd throw deep to Moss to try and get him 400 yards receiving and 6 touchdowns).

The game could be all consuming.

Full Madden seasons played out in dorm rooms, fraternity houses, and basements across America. You and your buddies would pick teams, argue over stats, and play entire schedules through the playoffs, tracking touchdowns and victories over the league's best defenses.

Nothing compared to the feeling of throwing a Hail Mary to beat your friend's Steelers squad or smashing through the line with Mike

Alstott for a first down when your pal would move Reggie White over three spots to plug the gap (yeah, I did that too).

And let's not forget the man himself: John Madden. With every "bam" and "whap" from the commentary, you felt like Madden and Pat Summerall were calling your game. And how did it all feel?

Boom!

#24

Adam Sandler

A dam Sandler, AKA The Sandman, has managed to dominate not one, not two, but four decades: the 90s, 2000s, 2010s, and now the 2020s. He's as timeless as a pair of Air Force 1s, an '86 Topps baseball card, or the *"you can do it!"* line from *The Waterboy*. And the 90s were where he truly cemented his status as the goofy, immature, king of silly and dumbass comedy for silly dumbasses (millions and millions of us).

First off, the *SNL* years. Yeah, we all remember Opera Man, and maybe you even caught a "Canteen Boy" sketch, but Sandler was on another level when it came to his songs. I'm talking about the *Lunch Lady Land* anthem, *The Hanukkah Song* (way back when there was only one version), and of course, *The Thanksgiving Song*. Sandler somehow became the holiday soundtrack to the lives of all of us in high school at the time. The thing was, if *SNL* was the appetizer, Sandler's solo albums were the hidden main course.

His breakout CD— *They're All Gonna Laugh at You!*—was quoted amongst your crew more than any line from a Seinfeld episode (yeah, I said it). Skits like *"Toll Booth Willie"* had kids and college bros laughing their heads off, laying the groundwork for Sandler's movie career, which would take him from sketch comedian to bonafide box office star.

Then came *Billy Madison*. A cult classic? Absolutely. Legendary? Yes. Chlorofil? More like bore-ofil!

But *Billy Madison* was just the start. *Happy Gilmore* followed soon after, and Sandler was officially running the comedy game.

By the time *The Waterboy, Big Daddy*, and *The Wedding Singer* rolled around, Sandler had established a new comedic empire. Maybe he wasn't breaking records like Jim Carrey, but Sandler's movies are still quoted today, and his style—somewhere between goofy and heartwarming—has stuck around for a reason.

So, while Mike Myers and Jim Carrey may have had a few more smash hits, The Sandman firmly planted himself in 90s lore, right where he belongs—at the top of the comedy food chain, duking it out with Bob Barker on a golf course where the price is wrong, bitch.

#23

Iron Mike Tyson

There are many phases to the saga of Iron Mike Tyson, and if you grew up in the 90s, you caught one of the wildest chapters. For some, Iron Mike was the ferocious knockout king of the 80s, a man who walked into the ring wearing nothing but a cut-off white towel and a death stare ready to destroy whoever was in his way.

If you were a kid back then, you spent hours as Little Mac, training to fight a 16-bit version of the man himself in *Mike Tyson's Punch-Out!!* on the NES, dodging Bald Bull and Soda Popinski, praying you had the code to face Tyson himself.

But for 90s kids, Tyson's story took a different turn. After his time in prison, he came back as a Pay-Per-View titan, though maybe not the invincible force of the 80s.

His first fight back was a spectacle against Hurricane Peter McNeely, a bout more about Tyson's return to the ring than the challenge at hand. I'm sure you remember that night. After months of posters and commercials saying "He's Back" in regards to Tyson, McNeely roared out of his corner, flailing and throwing haymakers that all missed. Tyson dropped him 10 seconds into the round and the whole thing was over in 89 seconds.

And then there was the infamous Evander Holyfield saga—culminating in *the* ear bite. None us will ever forget the slow motion replays of Tyson gnawing Holyfield's ear like a chicken McNugget. Gross. Also: captivating.

In the 90s, Tyson was a pay-per-view cash machine, almost synonymous with HBO boxing, delivering fights you had to see, just to find out what crazy shit might happen next.

It wasn't just about his punches anymore—though he still had them. It was about everything surrounding Tyson. The man was unpredictable, a walking quote machine for Larry Merchant. He'd drop lines that had your jaw on the floor, making Jim Lampley's commentary feel like the voice of reason amidst chaos.

Sure, Tyson never quite became the unbeatable monster of the 80s again, but that didn't matter. He was bigger, bulkier, and just as fascinating, even if his skills had faded a bit.

From a cultural standpoint, Tyson's 90s comeback gave us some of the most iconic (and mostly disappointing) fights of the decade. He certainly wasn't prime Iron Mike, but we're glad he didn't fade into Bolivian too soon.

#22

Georgetown
Iverson

When you think of Allen Iverson today, the image is vivid: Sixers jersey, cornrows, shooting sleeve, tats, all heart, and all speed—a fierce, relentless scorer and an undeniable icon. But before AI became "The Answer," before the crossover that broke ankles and rewrote the game, there was *Georgetown* Iverson.

Back when March Madness was packed with future NBA superstars playing two or three years before heading to the pros, we got to watch Allen Iverson 1.0, a fresh-faced flash of gray jersey who owned the college hoops spotlight.

Georgetown Iverson was so cool he made you want to go to Georgetown, an elite academic D.C. school you otherwise wouldn't have cared much about. He had the sleeveless cut off tee under the baggy uniform (which you tried to emulate and failed), the black wristbands on his left wrists (same) and a confidence that popped out of the television screen.

This wasn't some physically dominant monster like Shaq or a tall, lanky center like Marcus Camby built for basketball.

Iverson was barely six-foot and may have weighed 175 pounds wearing a backpack full of bricks, but he was straight-up lethal in the Big East—a conference that actually meant something in the 90s.

Iverson was captivating TV, a human pinball on the court, and every March Madness run was a showcase of his ability to torch defenses for 30 or 40 points.

Iverson was the guy everyone in the dorm or living room was hyped to see; he was a small, scrappy kid who looked like he could be your size, getting buckets like nobody's business. And Georgetown Iverson was far more than a run-of-the-mill college basketball star—he was a cultural touchstone.

Before the iconic Reebok deal, before AI became synonymous with hip-hop culture and the NBA, there was this uncut diamond of a player, carving up the Big East like a one-man army. Georgetown Iverson was the vibe before vibes were a thing—a one-of-one that changed college basketball forever.

#21

Basic Instinct

This essay is going to be a little different than the others because I have a very personal, very awesome story to tell you about *Basic Instinct*.

Here goes:

It's the summer of '92 and I'm visiting my grandparents solo in Florida. I'm 14. The main activities were the dog track, dinner at 5pm & movies with my grandfather. He wasn't into movies so he'd see whatever I wanted. This is all you need to know about how I hatched a devious plan – that turned disastrous.

The first thing to keep in mind about this story is this: We weren't seeing movies on opening weekend. No. My grandfather did not spend money on entertainment. We were hitting the Delray 6 Cineplex built in like 1958. $2 movie tickets for movies that had come out months earlier.

Now to point #2...

The movies available to me on this trip in the summer of '92 were the new releases that came out in the spring of '92. No opening weekends. These were movies (back then) caught in the dead period: 2 months out of the theater and 5 months from being at Blockbuster

So...

In the spring of '92 the ultimate "I want to see this but I'm too young but I'm a teenage boy how can I see this" movie came out: *Basic Instinct*

This is pre-internet. I was in 8th grade. I knew NOTHING about it other than Sharon Stone was hot and I heard you saw her naked...

So I float to my grandpa that we see *Basic Instinct*. I dance around the plot and why I'm excited to see it and I call it a "Michael Douglas" movie; the guy from Wall Street (which I also hadn't seen). My grandfather says fine - then out of nowhere asks my grandmother to come.

Whaaat?

Now I'm freaking out.

I don't know much about this movie, but I KNOW my grandmother shouldn't see it. Especially with me. But there wasn't anything I could do. I wanted to see it and couldn't think of a way to tell my papa that grammy shouldn't go...

So off we went...

The whole ride I'm half-giddy / half-terrified.

We pull up and get 3 tickets for $6. Get 3 popcorns for $3 and... The theater is PACKED. It's loaded with horny old dudes wanting to see Sharon Stone's boobs.

"This must be some picture," my grandmother says...

They wave to various friends as we try to find three seats. I'm mortified, realizing what's about to happen.

What have I done?

We end up in the 2nd row up front.

Me, jammed in between my grandfather and grandmother. I'm a sandwich of humiliation. Then the movie starts and things get 1,000 times worse.

I don't know if you remember the beginning of *Basic Instinct*.

But there's nudity. And sex. And more nudity. And I'm watching it. In public. Sitting between my grandparents... I wanted to disappear.

As the opening credits roll... And as the on the screen sex gets more intense... My grandfather blurts out so the whole theater can hear:

"You see that, Geraldine! We should have been actors!"

The line brings the house down. It was like a peak Chris Rock punchline. The entire room is hysterical

Then he says in a booming voice:

"You're not gonna believe this! But my grandson took us to see this picture! I should listen to him more often!"

Another wave of laughter rocks the theater. I wanted to shrink to nothing. I didn't know embarrassment could make you shake. But I was vibrating...

For the next 100 minutes or so I had to watch Sharon Stone's boobs ten feet tall on the big screen in the front row. Sitting between my grandparents. Red faced. Filled with regret. What a movie!

But here's the thing:

When I got home and told my buddies that I saw *Basic Instinct* in the theater... I was an instant legend. At least for a day or two.

That's how big this movie was.

And every single one of you reading this knows when you saw it, and where, and you remember *the scene*.

#20

The
'92 Dream Team

B ack in the days of athletic yore, professional athletes weren't
allowed to compete in the Olympics because being an amateur
and not being paid for your talents (while every other entity involved
got paid handsomely) was considered "honorable". Or something.

In hindsight, it's an absurd notion.

The Olympics are the world's biggest sports stage, and when it
came to team sports, most of the best players on the planet were stuck
at home because they chose to make the sport they were Olympic-level
good at their career.

But then came 1992, and everything changed. Pro athletes were
finally given the green light to compete, and the first sport everyone
knew would blow the doors off?

Basketball.

Specifically, USA basketball.

And even more specifically, the Dream Team.

If you were a hoops fan in the late '80s and early '90s, the Dream
Team was just that - a dream. More than your typical All-Star Game,
where guys tried hard for the final 10 minutes to win the MVP award.
This was basketball stardom on an epic scale, with every legend you

grew up idolizing rocking the same jersey, representing the good old USA.

And that roster?

I bet you can still rattle off those names like they're etched in stone: Jordan. Magic. Bird. Barkley. Ewing. Pippen. Stockton. Malone. Robinson. Mullin. Drexler. And, of course, Christian Laettner (should have been Shaq).

Everything about the Dream Team was iconic. You had the famous *Sports Illustrated* cover with Barkley, Ewing, Malone, Magic and Jordan. And you had the unforgettable *Newsweek Magazine* cover with Jordan dead center, flanked by Magic and Bird, like a still shot of the NBA's 80s and 90s Mount Olympus. You had Magic coming out of retirement after his HIV announcement, and Larry Bird's creaky back giving it one last go.

You remember the practice stories from Monte Carlo. Jordan, Magic, Bird—three alpha dogs leading separate squads in the most competitive scrimmages ever. Trash talking. One-upping. All. Day. Long.

And let's not forget the moments that became legendary. Barkley dunking so hard he practically broke the backboard, Magic and Bird passing like it was the '80s again, and of course, the Jordan-Reebok flag incident, where MJ draped the American flag over the Reebok logo because his loyalty to Nike was stronger than anything else.

Today, we take NBA stars in the Olympics for granted. But back in '92? The Dream Team was that rarity in sports - a true first. It was the ultimate flex that the U.S. didn't just have the best players, we had the greatest team ever assembled. No contest, no debate, just unadulterated world dominance. And it was awesome.

#19

Hot Pockets & Bagel Bites

As we've been establishing throughout this book, the 90s were dope. And in order for the decade to reach maximum dopeness, we needed the perfect foods to fuel us; to sustain us; to keep us going at all hours of the day or night as we dominated Madden, hyped ourselves up for driveway hoops, or scarfed down something quick to stay up for the end of *SmackDown*.

We needed something simple, fast, and loaded with meat, cheese, and bread in every flavor imaginable, ready to go in minutes. Enter: the ultimate duo—Hot Pockets and Bagel Bites.

These two culinary icons sat firmly at the top of the 90s food pyramid, ready in a pinch for every hunger emergency imaginable.

A boring night with nothing in the fridge? No problem.

Friends coming over on short notice? Covered.

Starving at midnight after finishing a season of NHL '94? Done.

No matter the starving scenario, a few minutes and a microwave later, you had a tasty Hot Pocket or a tray of crispy Bagel Bites, transforming your hunger into pure satisfaction.

Let's start with Hot Pockets: essentially mini calzone-like sandwiches filled with molten cheese and whatever else your 90s heart desired. Ham and swiss? Check. Pepperoni pizza? Check. Cheeseburger flavor? A breakfast version with eggs? Sure, why not?

The brilliance came with that patented little sleeve that ensured the entire Hot Pocket got heated through (no icy middle like those second-rate microwave burritos).

And if you were a Hot Pocket master, you knew the key to elevating your snack game—dipping them in ranch, ketchup, or even blue cheese. Suddenly, a late-night snack turned into a gourmet feast (sort of).

But the perfect sidekick?

Bagel Bites.

Tiny, cheesy little pizza bites on mini bagels that tested your warming ability. Cook them just right and you had crunchy little discs of perfection. Cook them too long and you get tiny hockey pucks. If you were an advanced warmer and had a little time, you could use the oven. Sure, it took longer, but the payoff was worth it. Golden, bubbly little bagels topped with gooey cheese and pepperoni - snack nirvana.

Whether you devoured Hot Pockets solo or paired them with a tray of Bagel Bites, these two were the ultimate power couple of 90s snacking. They fueled sleepovers, video game marathons, and everything in between. And honestly? We're all better for it.

In the end, the TV ad slogan was right:

When you want a hot meal, without a big deal: Hot Pockets.

#18

Point Break

Some movie premises are too good to be true, especially for us teenage dudes in the '90s. For the 98% of us who didn't live anywhere near a beach with year-round waves, surfing was already this mysterious, unattainable dream. Then, along comes a movie about surfing—and not just surfing, but *bank robbing* surfers.

That's a slam dunk idea before you even roll the cameras or write one word of the screenplay.

Ask any teenage dude (in the 90s or now) if he'd watch a movie where surfers rob banks, and you've got a resounding, "Hell yes!" on your hands.

Now, let's make it even more epic. What if the movie involved sending a cop undercover to bust this gang of wave-riding criminals? And what if that cop was cooler than a cop? What if he was an EFF! BEE! EYE! Agent?

And what if that agent was an ex-star college quarterback with a name that sounds like it belongs in the College Football Hall of Fame: Johnny Utah. Now you add in some skydiving, girls in bikinis, and an epic bromance, and you've got *Point Break*, a movie that was scientifically engineered to melt the mind of every teenage boy in America.

But a killer premise needs a killer cast. Enter Patrick Swayze as Bodhi, the spiritual, surf-loving, adrenaline-junkie leader, fresh off *Road*

House—the VHS movie your parents didn't let you watch but that you snuck in anyway. And then, there's Johnny Utah himself, played by Keanu Reeves. Yes, the same Keanu from *Bill and Ted's Excellent Adventure* who suddenly became the ultimate action star. Forget *The Matrix* or *John Wick*—his transformation began with *Point Break*.

The movie also has great utility when it comes to quotes. Whenever you're out and you're ordering two of anything, you can say, *"Utah! Gimme two!"*, to find any kindred spirits in ear shot.

And who hasn't said to their buddies when doing nearly any activity together with a new person: "You've got that Kamikaze look in your eyes... Be careful... He'll take you to the edge and past it."

And even if you've never surfed a day in your life, you have an opinion on the best big wave surf spots, specifically about whether Bells Beach Australia is bigger than Waimea in Hawaii.

Your opinion is obviously: "No way Bells is bigger than Waimea, bro!"

Bottom line: Point break has no CGI, no superheroes, no fantasy gimmicks— it's simply action perfection - and we're all better for having watched it at least 406 times on cable. Now don't start chanting.

#17

Saturday Night Live

Y ou know the names: Chris Farley, Phil Hartman, Dana Carvey, Mike Myers, Adam Sandler, Cheri Oteri, Rob Schneider, David Spade, Will Ferrell, Tim Meadows, Norm Macdonald, Kevin Nealon, Chris Rock and a half-dozen more.

In hindsight, it seems like so many of these cast members belonged to different eras, but ALL those eras overlapped in one decade: From Dana Carvey's 1990 peak to mid-90s Farley's dominance to Will Ferrell's late 90s masterpieces. The same decade launched the iconic skit of Phil Hartman jogging to McDonald's as Bill Clinton AND Will Ferrell as Alex Trebek on Celebrity Jeopardy!.

The roster of legendary skits say it all: The Chippendales Audition, The Roxbury Guys, Wayne's World. You may still drop an occasional "SCHWING!" without realizing it. You may still randomly yell, *"I live in a van, down by the river!"* You may demand that people know you drive a Dodge Stratus.

We had legends behind the update desk: Dennis Miller to start off the decade, followed by Kevin Nealon and the G.O.A.T, Norm.

We had Sandler's Thanksgiving and Hanukkah songs, which are now the de facto anthems of both holidays to this day - and this is to say nothing of his underground hit CD, *They're All Gonna Laugh at*

You. Bonus points to everyone who can still quote the entire Tollbooth Willy skit.

I know every generation claims *their Saturday Night Live* cast was the best. But in the '90s? It was the truth. The cast was stacked deeper than the old school McDonald's menu.

And we haven't even hit the movies from the SNL stars yet: *Wayne's World I & II, Billy Madison, Happy Gilmore, Tommy Boy, Night at the Roxbury, Coneheads, Austin Power I, II & III.*

Yeah, the '80s had Eddie Murphy, and the '70s had the OG legends like Bill Murray and Dan Aykroyd. But the '90s? That was when SNL transcended sketch comedy and became a factory for feature films, VHS tapes, and dorm-room classics made by cast members who were still in the cast (this is a big distinction by decade).

And that's the way it is.

RIP, Norm.

#16

NBA Jam

Let me paint the picture of a perfect Friday night in the '90s with your dude friends when you were 13. First, the sleepover. The parents drop you off, and the pizza order goes in—Domino's, obviously. You get a liter of Coke thrown in for free because it's the '90s and Domino's was all about those deals. Maybe they toss in some cookies, but your mom probably already stocked the pantry with EL Fudge, Toll House, Oreos, or classic Chips Ahoy. If you were really lucky, there were ice cream sandwiches in the freezer, ready for when things got serious.

The TV's ready, and somewhere in the house, there's a Nintendo hooked up. Maybe it's in your room—probably not. Maybe it's in the basement, or if you were really living large, a rec room or playroom. But as long as NBA Jam was loaded up, none of that mattered. You knew you were in for hours of unfiltered fun—dunking on each other, draining threes, blocking shots like your life depended on it.

You and your friends would pick a team and run it all night. Early '90s? Maybe you're rolling with Gary Payton, Shawn Kemp, and Detlef Schrempf. Maybe you're rocking Shaq and Penny, or the Knicks with Ewing, Oakley, and Starks. Either way, your squad had a big man, a three-point sniper, and a quick guard, and you were going to take it to the house.

And then, the moment. The three words that took your game to the next level: *He's heating up!*

But no, scratch that. The *real* moment, the peak of sleepover gaming glory, was when you heard:

He's on fire!

And once you heard the iconic *Boom-shaka-laka!* It was game on.

Full-court alley-oops, spinning dunks, epic blocks, trash-talking your friends—the full *NBA Jam* experience. Remember those days? They've never been topped.

#15

Stone Cold & The Rock

Y ou could write entire books about Stone Cold Steve Austin and The Rock—hell, they each deserve their own documentary series, maybe even their own monuments. These two aren't just Hall of Famers; they're legends, two of the four men who should be chiseled into wrestling's Mount Rushmore. For those of us who grew up in the '80s and '90s, who first fell in love with wrestling when Macho Man Randy Savage and Hulk Hogan dominated, and then drifted away in middle school, distracted by sports, girls, or school, there was one thing that pulled us back into the ring: the *Attitude Era*.

And at the center of that era were two icons: the Texas Rattlesnake, Stone Cold Steve Austin, and The Great One, The People's Champ, and now the Final Boss, The Rock. The *Attitude Era* was a wrestling juggernaut. It didn't just bring us back to the WWE—it redefined our generation. Sure, the late '80s and early '90s were great. We had legends like Bret Hart, Junkyard Dog, Hacksaw Jim Duggan, and of course, Hogan and Andre. But as much as we loved those characters, the golden era was PG at best.

Then came the *Attitude Era*, and everything changed. Gone were the cartoonish gimmicks and family-friendly storylines. In their place were beer chugging, trash-talking, middle-finger-throwing superstars who didn't just push the envelope—they ripped it apart. We had Stone Cold, flipping off his boss and smashing two beers together. We had The Rock, raising an eyebrow and cutting promos that crossed so many lines we lost track. They transcended the ring, becoming pop culture juggernauts and launching catch phrases that have become part of 90s dudes jargon to this day.

If you were in college back then, you didn't hit the bars until after *Friday Night Smackdown* ended and probably watched *Monday Night Raw* over *Monday Night Football*. You called your friends "jabronis" and told them to know their role and shut their mouths. It was a glorious time to be a wrestling fan. The *Attitude Era* was a true revolution. And at the heart of it? Stone Cold and The Rock, the two names you simply can't write the story of the '90s without. Long live the *Attitude Era*.

And if you think I'm overstating the importance of these two wrestling icons, I have one thing to say to you:

IT DOESN'T MATTER WHAT YOU THINK!

#14

Jurassic Park

E very kid grows up obsessed with dinosaurs: T-Rex, Triceratops, Brontosaurus. As a third or fourth grader, your life's dream was to somehow see a real live dinosaur.

Yes, there were cartoons (*Dino-Riders*) and odd sitcoms (*Dinosaurs*), coloring books, and a big entry in the encyclopedia Britannica that had some decent pics, but none of those were in the ballpark of what seeing an actual dinosaur would be like.

The closest we got to a realistic dinosaur was a crappy "life-sized" animatronic that we'd see at a museum on a field trip. Half the time it looked like the thing might malfunction and fall on you in a pile of gears and sparks.

Then in 1990, everything changed.

Michael Crichton released his novel, *Jurassic Park*, and suddenly, everyone—from science dorks to the cool kids—was reading a book with a dinosaur skeleton on the cover.

But that was just the beginning.

Word spread that Steven Spielberg, the guy who made *E.T.* and *Indiana Jones* and *Jaws*, was going to turn *Jurassic Park* into a movie using the most advanced CGI the world had ever seen.

And when the movie dropped in 1993?

Game over.

We were *the* generation to witness what CGI could really do—before *The Matrix*, before *Harry Potter,* before every Marvel superhero assembled. We saw a T-Rex on the big screen for the first time, and it was like being smacked in the face by the future of entertainment. *If they can make dinosaurs look real, what else can they do?*

Jurassic Park's opening weekend was a cultural event. Everyone had to see it. Kids, parents, grandparents—it didn't matter. You either saw *Jurassic Park*, or you were the poor soul who had to pretend you knew what "Clever girl" meant on Monday.

The CGI was mind-blowing, the dinosaurs were terrifying, and the plot? A theme park with real dinosaurs where everything goes wrong? I mean, come on!

It was the ultimate "What if?" of our childhoods brought to life. And the best part? It's still the gold standard for dino flicks. They've tried to reboot it, sequel it, and franchise it, but nothing's ever going to top the moment when that T-Rex roared for the first time with the "when dinosaurs ruled the earth" banner falling to the ground.

For one shining moment in 1993, *Jurassic Park* made us all believe in dinosaurs again—and it was awesome.

#13

Cindy Crawford

When I was 12 or 13 I'm 100% confident I didn't know what the word "supermodel" meant. Nor did I know what the word "smoldering" meant. But I knew Cindy Crawford was both. For many of us growing up in the '90s, she was the first pin-up we ever had. We were too young for Christie Brinkley and way too young for Farrah Fawcett or Bo Derek. But Cindy Crawford? She was ours.

She was *the* supermodel.

Her face (and body) was everywhere, from magazine covers to billboards to that unforgettable Super Bowl Pepsi commercial that became more iconic than the drink itself.

Every kid had that image of Cindy in jean shorts and a white tank top burned into their minds. Don't lie. You can picture it right now. And you're probably going to stop reading for a minute to find the commercial on YouTube. Then you'll go look for some of her *SI Swimsuit* Issue spreads. Go ahead. It's worth it. We'll wait right here.

Okay. You good? You get your old school Cindy Crawford fix?

While you're likely over 35 now, back in the day, when you were pining after your on-screen contemporaries—Tiffani-Amber Thiessen in *Saved by the Bell* or Topanga from *Boy Meets World,* or whoever you chose— you mostly stuck to girls your age who were cute and maybe attainable, but they weren't women yet.

Cindy Crawford? She was something else entirely. She was the embodiment of a horny teenaged dude's fantasy.

That beauty mark. The *Sports Illustrated* shoots. The bathing suits. The workout videos. The *Playboy* spreads. Even Denis Leary ranting about her in an MTV ad helped sear her into pop culture history.

For a time, Cindy Crawford stood alone at the top. Sure, others came for the crown later. Tyra Banks. Kathy Ireland. Elle MacPherson.

But there was only one Cindy Crawford, and for us, she was all we needed.

#12

Chris Farley

C hris Farley was the clown prince of the '90s. *Holy Schnikes, fat guy in a little coat. Tommy want wingy.* Chippendales. And who could forget, a van down by the river.

His impact was limitless, rippling through every living room tuned into *Saturday Night Live*, and then forever imprinted on college dorm walls with *Tommy Boy* posters.

Tommy Boy was his masterpiece, but he was more than that. There was something about him that wasn't just funny; it was real. He made you laugh because he made you *feel*. We *rooted* for him. We wanted to be his friend, and that was part of the magic.

During his apex, Farley was a human lightning bolt—an electrifying presence whose name alone made you smile. Every appearance, whether sprinting and cartwheeling down the aisles on *Letterman* or smashing through sketches on *SNL*, left you laughing your ass off. Sometimes he didn't have to say anything. The man could make you laugh with a look.

More than a comedian or actor; he was a touchstone for our entire generation. For those of us growing up in the '90s, with parents who'd wax nostalgic about the golden days of John Belushi, Farley was *our* guy. He idolized the greats, and we, in turn, idolized him.

Chris Farley was a one-man, real-life Three Stooges act. The kind of guy who could make you laugh so hard you'd have tears streaming down your face, but also someone who, deep down, made you want to hug him.

His legacy?

Laughter and joy.

Farley gave everything in every performance, and that's why we'll never forget him.

#11

Will Smith & The Fresh Prince of Bel-Air

"*N*ow *this is a story all about how my life got flipped-turned upside down...*"

These are the first lyrics of the *Fresh Prince of Bel-Air*'s theme song from its debut in September of 1990.

It's almost 35 years later and I guarantee most of you reading this can finish the verse:

"And I'd like to take a minute. Just sit right there. I'll tell you how I became the prince of a town called Bel-Air."

Simple. Brilliant.

In 2024 you know Will Smith as the Chris Rock-slapping, over-exposed-on-social-media, kinda-sorta still A-list actor.

But back in the day? When we were pre-teens and teens?

Will Smith was the *coolest dude on TV.*

In fact, before he even stepped foot on the set of a television show we had already memorized most of the lyrics to *"Parents Just Don't Understand"*.

Then came *Fresh Prince* starring the Fresh Prince, with Will Smith rocking Jordans, baggy clothes, neon hats and cracking jokes non-stop. We watched *Fresh Prince* because we kinda wanted to be the Fresh

Prince. We wanted a goofy brother like Carlton, a cool sister like Hilary and of course, a father figure like Uncle Phil, equal parts intimidation and love. We even wanted a best friend to have our own cool handshake with like Jazzy Jeff.

And even though most of us didn't attend a rich private school and probably didn't even own a blazer, if we did, you can bet we'd wear it inside out like Will.

By the show's sixth and final season in 1996, the rapper who joked about borrowing his parents' car and taking hits from Mike Tyson and talking to Freddie Kruger would become one of the biggest movie stars in the world.

Bad Boys. Independence Day. Men in Black. Enemy of the State.

And it all started with that kid from West Philadelphia, born and raised.

#10

Jerry Maguire

Fun fact: *Jerry Maguire* could have looked completely different. Imagine Tom Hanks as Jerry, Jamie Foxx as Rod Tidwell, and Gwyneth Paltrow as Dorothy Boyd. Weird, right? It's like picturing *Saved by the Bell* with Johnny Depp as Zack Morris. Different timeline, same 90s heart.

Crowe once said that *Jerry Maguire* came from a mix of real-life inspiration and pure fiction. The idea of agents going all-in for their clients came from guys like Rosenhaus, but the soul of the movie? That was Crowe and his late-night brainstorming with writer/producer James L. Brooks.

Over bad pizza, even worse coffee and a photo of Brian Bosworth with his agent, they imagined what would happen if a high-powered agent found his conscience—mid-career, mid-life, mid-90s.

Turns out, they were onto something.

Incredibly, *Maguire* manages to combine several genres that don't often collide with success: sports movie, chick flick, drama.

An argument can be made that Cameron Crowe's masterpiece is, in fact, all of these films. From the viewpoint of Dorothy Boyd, this movie is the ultimate chick flick: single mom with an adorable kid falls in love with a successful, handsome guy who is/was her boss.

From the viewpoint of Rod Tidwell, this is a sports movie about maturity and his NFL career.

And lastly, but most importantly, from the viewpoint of Jerry, this movie is a drama about his life before and after his famous mission statement.

All three storylines are powerful.

All three work.

And miraculously, they all work together.

Add in a killer lead soundtrack song with Bruce Springsteen's *'Secret Garden'*, complete with a radio play version that included quotes from the film, and you've got a near-perfect movie for... well... just about everyone.

Think about the lasting impact of this film.

We're nearly 30-years past its premiere in December 1996 and if you reference any of the big quotes:

"You had me at hello."

"Show me the money!"

"Help me help you!"

"You complete me."

I'd venture to say that 75% of the people around you over 35 will know exactly what you're talking about.

That's staying power. That's impact. That's the Quan.

#9

Seinfeld

S einfeld was - *and still is* - a pop culture juggernaut.

From *"I was in the pool!!!"* to *"Master of my Domain"* to *"the sea was angry that day my friends"* the references and quotes from the show still fly regularly among 40+-year-old dudes.

In real time, on Thursday nights back in the 90s, the show was like a cultural playbook of sorts, a guide on how to deal with every awkward situation life could throw at you.

If you weren't watching it live (because back in the stone age of twenty five years ago you couldn't tape anything without a VHS player and nobody could get those to record properly), you were a loser at school the next day, doomed to hear your friends shouting "No soup for you!" after swatting your shot in hoops - while you stood there, clueless, having no idea what they were referring to.

The brilliance of *Seinfeld* was how it turned mundane minutiae, as Elaine put it, into hall-of-fame-level comedy brilliance. This was a show that debated the etiquette of double-dipping a chip. Double. Dipping.

NOTE: you're lying if you haven't called out a buddy (or your own kid) on double dipping in the last twelve months.

And then you've got the legendary characters:

Our favorite marine biologist, George, who built a napping station under his desk and who once faked being handicapped to get a special bathroom at work. Who tried to have sex while also eating a pastrami sandwich. Who pushed women and children out of the way to escape a kitchen fire at a kid's birthday party. Who chased after Marissa Tomei because she loved quirky, bald men.

Jerry, our neurotic stand-in as a witness to his friends' lunacy. The puffy shirts, the white sneakers, the cereal, the man afraid of man hands.

Then we have the CEO of Kramerica Industries, Cosmo Kramer himself, the legend, the creator of "Festivus," the man who buttered himself up and cooked in the sun, who got cast in a Woody Allen movie by accident, and started a brief career as a Calvin Klein model because he was "avant-garde."

And finally we've got Elaine, the dry-heave dancing, sponge-worthy judging, nipple-on-a-card heart of the show.

Seinfeld had it all, from the famous "Soup Nazi"—a tyrant of broth who made you follow his bizarre ordering rules or face banishment from his restaurant: "No soup for you!"

Fun Fact: Back when I was in high school in New Jersey, we ditched class one day and went into NYC specifically to go to the Soup Nazi for lunch on 55th and 8th (I don't even remember what it's really called). The experience was fairly similar to the show, with a quick-moving line, little talking and abrupt ordering. I got the lobster bisque - it was tremendous.

We had entire episodes about how annoying it is to wait for a table at a Chinese restaurant, looking for cars in parking lots, smells in cars, parking cars and more.

Every episode was filled with these little moments that made you laugh and cringe because you saw yourself in them. You've dealt with close talkers, low talkers, people who "yada yada yada" over important details, and you knew exactly how irritating all of it could be - and still is - which is why Seinfeld remains a stalwart of pop culture to this day. Not that there's anything wrong with that.

#8

Shaq & Penny's Orlando Magic

When you were a kid did you even know where Orlando was? Yes, you probably knew it was in Florida and that Disney World was there, but outside of going to the Magic Kingdom, did you have any frame of reference for the actual city of Orlando?

Me neither.

Even when they got their NBA franchise in the '89 season most of us didn't care.

Then they drafted Shaquille O'Neal in 1992 and Penny Hardaway in 1993 and suddenly this random city in the middle of a random spot in Florida seemed like the coolest place ever. And their jerseys and shorts and hats - with the black and white stripes and the dripping stars - were instant "cool kid" apparel from coast to coast.

And it was all because of two unique dudes with unique names and unique charisma who took the NBA by storm. Then, for about four years, Shaq and Penny were a perfect combination of hoops talent and pop culture dominance, providing us with everything from *Inside Stuff* segments, ESPN highlights, Shaq rapping with Fu-Schnickens, and Penny's Lil' Penny puppet voiced by Chris Rock (see the Lil' Penny chapter). These two are part of the 90s decade's DNA.

Why?

Despite the fact that you've mostly seen Shaquille O'Neal in a suit and tie on TNT the last ten or fifteen years, do not forget for one second that he was a beast on the court.

At 7'1" and over 300 pounds, he treated real NBA rims like we treated those plastic Fisher-Price ones as kids. He cone literally brought down the entire backboard on live TV against the New Jersey Nets.

But it wasn't just his dominance in the paint that made Shaq stand out—he also happened to be everywhere. He dropped rap albums like *Shaq Diesel* (which went platinum), starred in movies like *Kazaam* (a noble effort), and showed up in weird video games like *Shaq Fu*.

Then there's smooth, understated Penny Hardaway.

Penny was effortlessly cool, the perfect counterbalance to Shaq's brute force play, with a handle and court vision that had people comparing him to Magic Johnson. And if you weren't glued to your TV for his highlights, you were talking about his Nike commercials and his sick Nike Air Penny shoes.

Often viewed as Shaq's sidekick or Robin to Shaq's Batman, don't forget that Penny was a 4x All-Star and 2x All-NBA First Team Selection.

Together, Shaq and Penny were a prime time duo— seemingly always on *NBA on NBC* or lighting it up in the playoffs. They were animated into episodes of *The Simpsons*, breaking out of the NBA bubble and into mainstream culture and they even starred in *Blue Chips* together as Neon Boudoux and Butch McRae.

Then when they led the Orlando Magic to the NBA Finals in 1995, it felt like the start of a dynasty. They took down Michael Jordan's Bulls (right after his return from baseball) in the playoffs, before losing to Hakeem Olajuwon and the Rockets in the Finals.

Though they'd never make it back to the Finals as teammates, with Shaq leaving to the Los Angeles Lakers, for a brief moment in time, Shaq & Penny (or Penny & Shaq) had the NBA in the palms of their giant hands.

#7

Sports
Illustrated

Sports Illustrated is dead and has been dead for a while. But these "always online" Zoomer-generation sports fans have no idea what they missed. I don't know the exact age and date cut-off. Maybe nobody under 30 remembers peak *SI*. Maybe it's 35.

Whatever the age, one thing is for sure and if you know, you know:

There was nothing like rolling home from school on a Wednesday or Thursday and grabbing that sweet, fresh issue of *Sports Illustrated* straight out of the mailbox...

Yeah, the physical mailbox. Tangible. In print & glorious.

As you'd pull down the flap of the box a million questions would race through your mind:

Who was on the cover?

What was Rick Reilly's column about?

Did Gary Smith write something?

What's Ralph Wiley covering?

Did Steve Rushin write from Greenland?

What about Jackie Mac? Or Gammons? Or Pearlman?

Do we know any of the Faces in the Crowd?

I'm telling you... every *SI* mail day was an event. Titans wrote for the magazine. Legends were on the cover. New voices wrote new stories.

If your favorite team or player had a feature it felt like you won something.

You'd read the whole thing, always back to front, because of Reilly.

You looked forward to the preseason rankings. You'd argue about who should be on the cover during the playoffs or after a championship or major. You'd be fired up for the March Madness breakdown, the NFL preview, the Sportsman of the Year.

And I can tell you firsthand that getting the swimsuit issue in the middle of a cold, barren New England winter was a mini-holiday for millions of dudes. Supermodels in bikinis on beaches while we were still bundled up and freezing? Absolutely genius move, *SI*.

If you were a sports fan in the 70s, 80s and 90s, *Sports Illustrated* was a mainstay in your house and your life.

Not only did we have the weekly issues, but we had the commemorative issues, the goofy sweatshirt giveaways, the windbreaker giveaways and of course, the legendary SI football phone when you signed up for like $60/year.

We had it all and the magazine flat out mattered.

The writing, the photos, the covers, the feel of it...

It spoke to millions of us. It meant something.

It was a weekly shared conversation for a generation of us.

You could walk into any group of dudes in school, at the basketball court, at the mall, wherever... and just say, "you see *SI* this week?"... and you'd have a 30 minute conversation.

That time has long passed.

But what a time it was.

And now it's gone.

RIP, *Sports Illustrated*.

#6

Mike Meyers & Dana Carvey

My first inclination was to separate Dana Carvey and Mike Myers. They both have a strong enough body of work to stand on their own. They have the movies, the star power and the crossover appeal out of comedy and into pop culture. But whenever I tried to rank each comedian I kept coming back to *Wayne's World*, the skits and the movie.

Even if we give each of them 50% of the credit for the success of the film, which we should, the weight of *Wayne's World* is so much heavier than their other work. And yes, we'll get to *Austin Powers* in a second, but there is no *Austin Powers* without *Wayne's World*. The order matters.

At first glance, the *Austin Powers* phenomenon should put Meyers a notch above Carvey, but here's my case for Dana Carvey being on equal footing:

Carvey was one-half of *Wayne's World*, but I'd argue the funnier half. In addition, Carvey was a Top 5 SNL talent of all time. During the 90s he had breakout character after breakout character, from Hans and Franz, to the Church Lady, to playing 2 different candidates during an election (George HW Bush and Ross Perot) to doing a spot-on Johnny Carson when Carson was king.

So, yeah, Carvey belongs.

The only Mike Myers skit that crossed over to the extent of Carvey's was his *Coffee Talk with Linda Richman*. He had a few others that you might remember, but none of them reached Hans and Franz level.

The movies, though...

This is where Meyers stakes his claim.

Like Carvey, he has *Wayne's World* and *Wayne's World 2*.

But he also has the cult hit, *So, I Married an Ax Murderer*. If you know, you know. And I realize that many of you don't, but for a certain segment of readers, this movie was brilliant. "Heed, Pants, Neowww!!"

Then, of course, we have *Austin Powers: International Man of Mystery* in 1997 and *Austin Powers: The Spy Who Shagged Me* in 1999, which made over $200 million at the box office. Powers was a phenomenon that gave us not only the title character, but also the ever-quotable Dr. Evil. The lines that we repeat from these movies to this day are impressive.

This gives Meyers two 90s movie franchises, two quotable big screen movie characters and one small screen breakout character to Carvey's one franchise, half-dozen small screen breakout characters and a few stand-up specials. Final verdict: TIE.

This tie, however, was a win for all of us who grew up in this decade. Not only did we get all the SNL laughs, we got every *Wayne's World* catchphrase:

"Schwiiing!"

"Not!"

"Psycho hose beast."

"Gun rack."

"Way!"

And on and on and on.

Then we got all the Austin Powers catchphrases:

"Oh, behave!"

"Yeah, baby!"

"One. Million. Dollars..."

Now think about all of the conversations you had with your buddies in the mid-nineties. There's at least a 55% chance that someone in the group said, "not!" or "yeah, baby!" at some point in the discussion when you were screwing around.

That's staying power. And that's the 90s.

#5

Baseball Cards

F orget crypto. Forget NFTs. Even forget the stock market.

If you're reading this and you came of age during the baseball card boom from the 1980s into the mid 1990s, the only education in economics you needed wasn't going to be found in a textbook or a class at school. Nope. Everything you needed to know came wrapped in a 2.5" x 3.5" wax pack full of sports cards.

When we were kids they held promise, future fortunes and they cost $.50/pack. You could hit up any grocery store, convenience store, pharmacy, 7-11 and if you had a dollar in your pocket you were baseball card rich:

Cards. Gum. Assets.

The kids today have no idea.

Back in 1992 there were no box breaks or buy-ins or $49.99 or $99 packs or $1,000 packs or $10,000 "One & One" Panini Treasure sets or live streams to see other cards or dozens of different sets with holograms and refractors and subtle variations or uniform slivers cut inside...

HELL NO.

We had cardboard. And three ring binders. And plastic sleeves...

We had a 4-pound Beckett guide that was our bible.

We coveted like 7 rookie cards:

Rickey Henderson

Don Mattingly

Kirby Puckett

Roger Clemens

Doc Gooden

Mark McGwire

Ozzie Smith

And then, of course, we overloaded on Ken Griffey Jr...

But for about 6 years we treated our card collection like it was our personal hedge fund.

We'd trade cards in the school cafeteria like stock brokers...

3 Frank Violas and 2 Ryne Sandbergs for a Jose Canseco Rookie

1 Jack McDowell RC plus 1 Ruben Sierra RC for a Benito Santiago rookie

We'd try to get lucky by loading up on Ellis Burks or Jim Abbott rookies. We took shots, cornering the market on random players with upside like Todd Benzinger and Walt Weiss or personal favorites like Oil Can Boyd...

And on and on we'd go, thinking that once we had the rookie cards from the entire '94 all-star team or all of the rookie cards from the '92 Sox or Yankees or A's that we could then put our cards in a vault for thirty years...

Then we'd open that vault up in 2024 when we were 40 and we'd... BE... RICH!!!

We know now that it wasn't meant to be.

But damn. What a time to be a kid. What a time to be alive. It was awesome.

If you're nodding your head with Topps & Fleer-filled nostalgia, then you know exactly what I mean.

#4

Jim Carrey

T he year is 1994.

Hollywood is ruled by a fleet of all-time A-List players fresh off a Hall of Fame year for movies in 1993. Steven Spielberg's *Jurassic Park* made nearly $400 million. Tom Cruise headlined *The Firm,* Harrison Ford starred in *The Fugitive,* Tom Hanks raked in cash in *Sleepless in Seattle* and was set to release *Forrest Gump.* Robin Williams was *Mrs. Doubtfire.* Denzel Washington and Julia Roberts starred in *The Pelican Brief.* Even Clint Eastwood had a smash hit with *In the Line of Fire.*

And those are just the blockbuster movies box office-wise.

Pop culturally, we got Jack Nicholson's incredible Colonel Nathan Jessup and Cruise again in *A Few Good Men,* Al Pacino in *The Scent of a Woman,* Sylvester Stallone in *Demolition Man* AND *Cliffhanger.* Even Bill Murray made the beloved *Groundhog Day.*

And yet...

1994 belonged to none of them.

If you were a gambling man on December 31, 1993 and a bookie said to you, "Here's a prop bet. Which actor's movies will gross the most money worldwide in 1994?" Then they gave you this list with the following odds:

Tom Cruise 4-1

Tom Hanks 6-1

Harrison Ford 7-1

Julia Roberts 8-1

Denzel Washington 10-1

Sylvester Stallone 15-1

Arnold Schwarzegger 20-1

White guy on *In Living Color* 10,000-1

Unless you're a liar, none of you would waste even $5 on the white guy from *In Living Color*, AKA, Jim Carrey. The reason I'm describing him as "the white guy from *In Living Color*" is to stress that up until 1994, that's how a vast, vast, vast majority of the television and movie watching public would have referred to Jim Carrey, if they referred to him at all.

Then, on February 4th, 1994, a comedy comet named *Ace Ventura: Pet Detective* hit theaters and altered the American pop culture landscape forever. Within weeks, millions of teenagers, to their parents' and teachers' chagrin, would be quoting the lunatic animal gumshoe nonstop:

Alllllllriiiiightyyyyy, then!

La-whooooo!!! Za-herrrrrr!

Finkle is Einhorn! Einhorn is Finkle!

In the end, the film made $107 million worldwide and exited the theaters just in time for Jim Carrey's OTHER '94 comedy to debut on July 28th: *The Mask*.

The Mask, co-starring a young Cameron Diaz, was a family friendly comedy that showcased Carrey's physical and verbal gifts perfectly. The movie had dance numbers, cartoon effects, and enough energy exuding off the screen to power the theater it was in. Like *Ace,* it also had catch phrases:

Someboooodyyyy stop me!!!!

Smmmmmmooookin'!!!!

And like *Ace,* was also a surprise hit, bringing in $352 million worldwide and leaving the theaters just in time for Jim Carrey's OTHER, OTHER '94 comedy to debut on December 16th, 1994: *Dumb & Dumber.*

If you're reading this book, this movie needs no introduction.

Directed by the Farrelly brothers.

Co-starring Jeff Daniels.

It's a masterpiece.

And yeah, you can triple check it...

Dumb & Dumber also came out in 1994 and cruised to a global box office of $247 million when the run ended in early 1995.

To save you the trouble of doing addition in your head or opening up the calculator app on your phone, Carrey's tally between *Ace, Mask* and *Dumber* was a ridiculous $706 million dollars globally.

All from the white guy from *In Living Color.*

The three movies catapulted Carrey to a level of fame typically reserved for action stars, Oscar-winning leading men, breakout *Saturday Night Live* comedians and hall of fame-level athletes. While Carrey didn't have a jersey for fans to wear, he had a dozen catchphrases to quote, outfits to copy for Halloween and movies to rent from Blockbuster the day they came out.

He'd gone from earning $25,000 per episode of *In Living Color* to $25M per movie. And then he really took off. The sequel to *Pet Detective, When Nature Calls,* earned double the box office of the original in 1995. Then he played the Riddler in *Batman Forever* later that year, stealing the entire movie from Val Kilmer and Tommy Lee Jones.

The Cable Guy broke $100 million. *Liar Liar* was a monster in 1997, earning $303 million, followed by the *Truman Show's* $264 million in 1998.

By the end of the decade, Carrey's movies made over $1.5 billion dollars at the box office. Not to mention about a dozen lights out performances at the MTV Video Movie Awards and a still-classic SNL hosting gig in 1996.

In short, Carrey not only owned big budget, high concept comedies in the 90s, he was one of a handful of movie stars whose name on the poster instantly meant $100 million at the box office. Easy choice for #1 comedian of the 90s.

I believe Jim Carrey should have been nominated for an Oscar for *Liar Liar.* The level of difficulty for that movie - where he had to act against the act of lying, and convince people he physically could not lie, was astonishing. Not a single other comedian or actor could have pulled that off. His performance is genius. And brilliant. And has a ton of heart. Watch it again. You'll see.

#3

Ken Griffey Jr.

I wrote this to kick off my Ken Griffey Jr. chapter in my book, *1996: A Biography*, and it still holds true:

You take a grown man who grew up loving baseball in the '80s and '90s and bring him to the Museum of Modern Art and ask him to describe a masterpiece by Van Gogh or Monet or Pollack and you'll likely get a shrug and an answer somewhere along the lines of, "eh, it's just paint."

Now you take that same man, sit him down and ask him to describe Ken Griffey Junior's swing and there's a damn good chance he might get a tear in his eye while he runs out of adjectives.

Beautiful. Pretty. Gorgeous. Sweet. Perfect. A work of art. Majestic. Graceful. Poetic. Breathtaking. Mesmerizing. Spectacular. Belongs in the Louvre. Magnificent. Spellbinding.

A man might not describe his own wife or daughter this way, but get him going on the subject of Griffey's swing and all of a sudden he's a cross between a thesaurus and Don Quixote. Such is the power of the most effortless, efficient, exquisite (see, I'm doing it now) baseball swing in the history of man.

But there's a reason we speak of Ken Griffey Jr. this way. His swing, his style and his charisma evoke a different time period than the one we live in now. To look at Griffey was to be carefree. To feel joy in doing something. To have swagger before swagger became 'swag' and then 'rizz and whatever comes next.

Ken Griffey Jr., with his magnetic smile and backwards hat and Rock 'N Jock laughs and home run derby performances and diving catches was more than a sequence of highlights or dazzling plays.

He was, as everyone would say now, a vibe.

More than Jordan. More than Gretzky. More than Tiger.

More than whatever other 90s icon you're thinking about.

To be a kid in the time when "The Kid" ruled baseball and baseball was still relevant was to grow up in a good mood. The "feel" of the Griffey era is something we've still not seen since. There are moments of Steph Curry's career that come close, as a new era of young hoopers chuck threes and mimic his celebrations, but nobody cares about Steph's shoes. And Steph doesn't have a signature look that we could copy.

But Griffey?

All you had to do was twist your hat backwards as a kid in the 90s and you instantly felt more confident; comfortable; cool.

That's why this book is called Generation Griffey.

Because while MJ was undoubtedly a bigger "star" than Junior was, Griffey defines the way we 90s grade schoolers and middle schoolers and high schoolers felt back then:

We were happy-go-lucky, backwards-hat-wearing, fun-loving kids... just like The Kid himself.

#2

Michael Jordan

*"**S**ometimes I dream, that he is me,*
You've got to see that's how I dream to be,
I dream I move, I dream I groove,
Like Mike,
Oh, if I could be Like Mike..."

There is now a 100% chance that you're smiling and singing this song out loud and humming "ba bum bum bum"... You're picturing the Gatorade commercial right now, with Michael Jordan smiling and chugging Citrus Cooler and bouncing the ball over that group of kids and laughing it up. You likely remember every frame of the commercial (which we cover in a different section of this book).

Now here's something to keep in mind: that commercial debuted in August of 1991. Over three decades ago!

How many things from three decades ago: a person, an event, a song, anything... can instantly make you happy and nostalgic for an entire period of your life?

Whatever is on that list, it's short, and if you grew up a sports fan in the 80s or 90s, Michael Jordan is at the top of the list. He is THE singular star of the decade and the entire MJ ecosystem is an exercise in peak 90s nostalgia.

From the commercials:

Gatorade, McDonald's, Hanes, Wheaties, Nike

To entertainment:

Space Jam, SNL Host, Michael Jackson's Jam video

To gear:

Air Jordans, the Jumpman logo, endless T-shirts, shorts, hats, hoodies

To, oh yeah, BASKETBALL:

6x Champion, 6x Finals MVP, 5x League MVP, 14x All-Star, 10x Scoring Champ, the '92 Dream Team, slam dunk champion and on and on...

And here's a unique stat:

Back when *Sports Illustrated* mattered and being on the cover was a HUGE DEAL, Michael Jordan appeared on the cover 50 times. That's nearly an entire year's worth of issues with one person on the front of the magazine. Muhammad Ali is second with 40 and LeBron James is third with 36.

It's impossible to describe how much the cover meant to readers who don't buy magazines anymore, but if you were on the cover your face was in people's inboxes - they're actual, in real life mail boxes - that week. And at its peak *Sports Illustrated* reached over 3 million readers weekly. Couple that with Jordan's highlights ruling SportsCenter (long before social media existed for highlights) and Jordan was the most popular person in sports in both print and television, the two biggest platforms of the day. That he also starred in a hit movie, *Space Jam*, is only icing on the cake.

In terms of 90s impact and influence, there's Michael Jordan and then everyone else.

#1

Classic SportsCenter

D ads and 90s kids, here's a fact:

We had it so good with SportsCenter and we didn't know it.... How could we?

We didn't know what was on the horizon that would try to take it down: first, league passes and TiVo and DirecTV... then the Internet and social media and YouTube...

During that brief, bright spot in sports media in the 1990s, Sports-Center was the best, coolest and most fun way to get the day's highlights...

We had black and white photos and box scores and features in the newspaper...

We had brilliant writing and reporting and pictures in *Sports Illustrated* and *Sporting News* and *ESPN: The Magazine*...

But for the big sports news of the day, the awesome plays and the clips from that night's games, nothing came close...

To watch Ken Griffey Jr. make a diving catch or Jordan hit a game winner or Barry Sanders twirl through a defensive line...

If you didn't catch it live, the only way to see it was on SportsCenter (maybe your local news sports show - maybe)...

And into this void stepped Dan Patrick and Keith Olbermann and Stuart Scott and Rich Eisen and Craig Kilborn and Linda Cohn and Robin Roberts and crew...

And all the catchphrases every kid in high school and college would repeat: "cool as the other side of the pillow"... Jumanji... En Fuego....

We'd watch SportsCenter at night then again in the morning.

It was a monolith. You'd show up at school and you'd have the same frame of reference for the highlights you saw. It was a shared experience.

It was tremendous And even though the show still exists and works, it's not a cultural touchstone anymore... It can't be... Not with every highlight available from 1,000 sources across social media instantly...

And there are bright spots to be sure...

But classic SC, man. It was a shared experience. By everyone. These kids don't know... Sitting there, retweeting highlights, sharing reels, scrolling their feeds... Doing the work to find what they like with no commentary or context.

Times change. I get it. And we always glorify what we grew up on. Maybe that's all this is.

But this is our book - a book for the Griffey Generation - and if we have to pick the *ONE* thing that united sports and pop culture and all of us, it would be SportsCenter.

And we all miss Stu Scott. He ruled.

Boo-Yah!

Final Cuts

A Word on Ranking Things

O kay... What'd I miss?

If you just finished this book, first, thank you for reading and I hope you enjoyed it and that it was a fun, nostalgic trip back to the 90s.

Second, I know there's stuff that you're thinking, "Dude! How did you leave off...."

And before you list those things, I'm sure I know some of them, so let me give you some loose thoughts on why I included certain things and not others.

Some things that I personally would have included I ended up leaving out because they felt too regional. For instance, Nomar Garciaparra. I loved Nomah! He was the face of my Red Sox for much of the 90s. BUT, were 90s dudes in San Antonio or Madison or Phoenix or San Jose talking about Nomar? Probably not. Same with Pedro Martinez... And for those 90s New Jersey Nets teams with Drazen Petrovic (RIP), Kenny Anderson and Derrick Coleman. I loved those guys, but they never crossed over to become a national phenomenon, like, say, those Sonics team with Payton & Kemp, which get a chapter in this book.

So if your local favorite 90s athlete, who may have made a bunch of All-Star teams or even be a Hall of Famer isn't in here, then that's likely why.

And then there are guys who definitely were relevant in the 90s, but for one reason or another felt like they belonged more to the 80s generation (at least to me), so I left them off. Guys like Jerry Rice. Guys like Rickey Henderson. Guys like Dominique Wilkins. Guys like Wayne Gretzky. Yes, they were still at the top of their game in the early 90s, but they felt like they belonged to the decade before.

Those are some of the thoughts I had regarding sports.

When it came to pop culture, music and "things", I went with my gut. Some things seemed to transcend the mission of the book (90s dude things).

Biggie & Tupac, for instance, were absolutely important to 90s dudes, but also to anyone who liked rap or hip hop and their legacy seems to bleed out well into the 2000s and today. Juxtapose that with Dr. Dre's "The Chronic", which very much placed my brain firmly into 1993. It feels much more *of the 90s*. When you see the cover or hear Let Me Ride, it takes you back to that moment.

Does that make sense? Yes? No? I know it's fuzzy logic, but this isn't trigonometry, so it's the best I've got.

Lastly, we're all different people from different places. I spent the early 90s in Shrewsbury, Massachusetts and the mid-90s in high school in New Jersey and the late 90s in college in Virginia. While I think "most" of the things in this book were relevant to a lot of us 90s dudes, I'm confident that if you grew up in Hermosa Beach, California in the early 90s and then went to high school in Dallas, Texas, or if you went to middle school and high school in a big city or a small town somewhere, you'd have a bunch of things that resonated with you or were more important to you from the 90s than they are with me.

Even so, I'd love to hear from you. What was your favorite chapter? Where did you disagree with the rankings? What'd I nail? What'd I miss?

Hit me up on Instagram or Twitter/X: @Jon_Finkel.

And the best place to write me is always by subscribing to my Books & Biceps newsletter at jonfinkel.com.

Appreciate you taking this trip back to our childhood with me!

90s Forever,

Jon

www.ingramcontent.com/pod-product-compliance
Lightning Source LLC
Chambersburg PA
CBHW021226090426
42740CB00006B/408